THE COLD WAR CHRONICLES

The Marshall Plan and the Truman Doctrine

George Capaccio

Cavendish Square
New York

Published in 2018 by Cavendish Square Publishing, LLC
243 5th Avenue, Suite 136, New York, NY 10016

First Edition

Library of Congress Cataloging-in-Publication Data

Names: Capaccio, George.
Title: The Marshall Plan and the Truman Doctrine / George Capaccio.
Description: New York : Cavendish Square Publishing, 2018. | Series: The Cold War chronicles | Includes index.
Identifiers: ISBN 9781502627315 (library bound) | ISBN 9781502627230 (ebook)
Subjects: LCSH: Marshall Plan--Juvenile literature. | Economic assistance, American--Europe--History--20th century--Juvenile literature. | Europe--Economic conditions--1945---Juvenile literature.
Classification: LCC HC240.K55 2018 | DDC 338.91'730409045--dc23

Editorial Director: David McNamara
Editor: Jodyanne Benson
Copy Editor: Rebecca Rohan
Associate Art Director: Amy Greenan
Designer: Alan Sliwinski
Production Coordinator: Karol Szymczuk
Photo Research: J8 Media

The photographs in this book are used by permission and through the courtesy of: Cover MPI/Archive Photos/Getty Images; p. 4 Reijn Dirksen, published Economic Cooperation Administration/Wikimedia Commons/File:Europe Plan Marshall. Poster 1947.JPG/Public Domain; p. 10 STF/AFP/Getty Images; p. 12 Universal History Archive/UIG/Getty Images; p. 14, 30, 35, 45, 47, 50, 55, 57, 66 Bettmann/Getty Images; p. 18 Lt. Victor Jorgensen/NARA/Wikimedia Commons/File:Kissing the War Goodbye.jpg/Public Domain; p. 20 H. F. Davis/Topical Press Agency/Getty Images; p. 26 Peteri/Shutterstock.com; p. 29 Harry S. Truman Library; p. 32 Wikimedia Commons/Bundesarchiv, Bild 101I-164-0389-23A/Theodor Scheerer/CC-BY-SA 3.0; p. 38 Felix Koch/Cincinnati Museum Center/Getty Images; p. 48 Harris & Ewing/LOC/Wikimedia Commons/File:Herbert Clark Hoover.jpg/Public Domain; p. 58 Interim Archives/Getty Images; p. 62 Sueddeutsche Zeitung Photo/Alamy Stock Photo; p. 70 Averell Harriman Papers, Manuscript Division, Library of Congress; p. 73 Byron Rollins/AP Images; p. 75 Yale Joel/The LIFE Picture Collection/Getty Images; p. 79 Edward Miller/Keystone/Getty Images; p. 81 Keystone-France/Gamma-Keystone via Getty Images; p. 84 Sergey Borisov/Alamy Stock Photo; p. 87 Ann Ronan Pictures/Print Collector/Getty Images; p. 89 E. Spreckmeester/Economic Cooperation Administration/Wikimedia Commons/File:Marshall Plan poster.JPG/Public Domain; p. 92 OFF/AFP/Getty Images.

Printed in the United States of America

CONTENTS

Introduction: Planning Europe's Postwar Recovery 5

1 Mounting Tensions 11

2 The Marshall Plan and the Truman Doctrine 27

3 The Faces of the Cold War 51

4 Negotiation and Innovation 71

5 The Legacy of the Marshall Plan and the Truman Doctrine 85

Chronology 99

Glossary 102

Bibliography 106

Further Information 108

Index 110

About the Author 112

To promote the Marshall Plan, an intra-European poster competition was held in 1950. This poster was one of the twenty-five most outstanding posters chosen.

Planning Europe's Postwar Recovery

Journalists are once again talking about the Cold War. Only now, they're not referring to the original Cold War but to what they see as a return to the mutual suspicions and rivalry that defined the long conflict between the United States and the Union of Soviet Socialist Republics (USSR). Fortunately, that conflict never turned into overt "hot" war. Had this come to pass, there is every likelihood the two superpowers, armed with nuclear weapons, would have succeeded not only in annihilating each other but in making much of the planet uninhabitable for centuries. Besides blanketing Earth with a sunlight-blocking cloud of ash and causing what scientists call a "nuclear winter," radioactive fallout from the detonation of nuclear warheads would have produced a pandemic of cancers affecting much of the human race and the entire animal kingdom.

Remembering the Cold War

According to a widely held view among historians, the Cold War lasted from roughly 1945 to 1989. In 1989, the USSR decided it could no longer afford to continue its ongoing rivalry with the United States over access to natural resources, control of third-world economic and political systems, and domination of its own sphere of influence, which included much of Eastern Europe. In a stunning capitulation that left the United States as the world's sole remaining superpower, the USSR relaxed its seventy-year-long commitment to the advancement of Communist ideology abroad. Within its own national borders, the USSR had developed a political system intended to compete with and ultimately defeat the capitalist, free-market model favored by the United States. The leaders of the USSR hoped to achieve their goals not necessarily through overt aggression but rather through influencing the governments of targeted countries by supporting political parties aligned with Communist values and ideals.

The USSR did not come into existence until 1922, five years after the Russian people revolted against the oppressive regime of Czar Nicholas II and ended three centuries of imperial rule. The October Revolution of 1917 brought into power Vladimir Lenin, a revolutionary thinker and visionary leader determined to transform the former Russian empire into the world's first nation founded on Communist principles. In response to the abdication of the Czar and the turmoil that soon engulfed Russia, the West decided to intervene.

For some historians, the armed invasion of Russia in 1918 marked the actual start of the Cold War. What followed were decades of conflict—conflict that on more than one occasion came dangerously close to a catastrophic, full-blown war. Other historians contend that the Cold War began soon after World War II ended in 1945. World War II started in 1939 when Germany, under Adolf Hitler, leader of the Nazi Party, invaded Poland. The Soviet Union fought on the side of the **Allies**, including France, Great Britain, the United States, Belgium, and Canada. The war was perhaps the bloodiest and most expensive and destructive war in history. About eighty-five million people were killed, and another sixty million became refugees. After six years of fighting, countries in Europe lay in ruins, with transportation and communication systems destroyed, buildings and monuments reduced to rubble, and many roads and highways impassable. Worse still were the tremendous loss of life and the poverty that engulfed much of Europe after the war.

The Major Conferences

In the pivotal year of 1945, the Allies held two conferences to plan the reconstruction of Europe and negotiate the roles of the three most powerful victors: the United States, Great Britain, and the Soviet Union. The first conference was attended by the "Big Three" wartime leaders: Joseph Stalin, Soviet dictator; Winston Churchill, British prime minister; and Franklin D. Roosevelt, United States president. This conference was held in Yalta, Ukraine, before Germany's surrender. Shortly after the Yalta Conference, President Roosevelt suffered a fatal stroke, and his vice president and successor, Harry Truman, joined the other leaders in

Potsdam, Germany when the war in Europe was over. With Germany's defeat, the alliance between the Soviet Union and the West began to fracture. Each side had its own vision of what a reconstituted Europe would look like and how to manage postwar Germany.

Despite their conflicting interests, the Big Three leaders succeeded in resolving several major issues at the conference in Potsdam, most notably the fate of Germany, which would be totally disarmed and demilitarized and divided into four occupation zones. Following the conference, relationships between Soviet Russia and the West became increasingly antagonistic as each side sought to expand its own sphere of influence in Europe and establish political and economic systems consistent with each side's ideology.

The Marshall Plan

In response to the devastation that stretched across Europe and affected millions of people, US officials proposed a comprehensive program of support known as the **Marshall Plan**, named after Secretary of State George Marshall. In this book, we'll explore the Marshall Plan in terms of its accomplishments and the part it played in the early years of the Cold War. In particular, we'll consider the role of the Marshall Plan in blunting the edge of Soviet influence in Western Europe. The Truman administration feared that the Soviet Union would seek to infiltrate and eventually dominate Western European governments, forcing them to adapt Communist as opposed to capitalist values. Was the Marshall Plan an unselfish, humanitarian effort on the part of the Americans to help Europeans overcome the consequences of the war and rebuild their economies? Or was it a continuation of America's anti-Communism that began with the United States' intervention in the 1918 Russian Revolution?

The Truman Doctrine

On March 12, 1947, President Harry Truman, in an address to Congress, stated that the United States must play a far more active role in containing the spread of **Communism**. He urged Congress to authorize substantial military and financial aid for European countries threatened by **subversive** elements. The principles he set forth in this speech later became known as the **Truman Doctrine**. It was one of the earliest formulations of Cold War policies the United States would pursue for the next four decades. The Marshall Plan, announced in June 1947, emerged as the first and most dramatic effort to turn the Truman Doctrine into facts on the ground.

In the chapters that follow, we'll look at the contributions and careers of people responsible for the development and implementation of the Marshall Plan. In addition to President Truman and Secretary of State George Marshall, our focus will include George Kennan, the American ambassador in Moscow, and former United States president Herbert Hoover. His detailed reports on the dire humanitarian situation in postwar Europe helped convince Truman that America urgently needed to reevaluate and restructure its aid program. One result of Hoover's recommendations was the Marshall Plan.

On May 7, 1945, in Reims, France, Germany officially surrendered to the Allies. General Alfred Jodl was the only German officer authorized to sign the surrender documents.

CHAPTER ONE

Mounting Tensions

The war in Europe officially ended on May 8, 1945, when Germany surrendered to the Allied powers. With the fighting over, the US Army had to plan a way of managing the hundreds of thousands of soldiers under its jurisdiction. To handle this challenge, military officials devised a point system based on how long each soldier had served and their combat experience. Using this system, soldiers were either sent to the Pacific to continue the fight against the Japanese, kept in Europe as part of the occupation force, or sent home to return to civilian life.

Patsy Giacchi

Patsy Giacchi, an Italian American soldier from Hackensack, New Jersey, was among those who were discharged from the army and sent home. He was drafted when he was eighteen years old. A few years later, he found himself on the beaches of Normandy, France, where his job was to

On June 6, 1944, Allied troops landed on the coast of Normandy, France, to liberate Europe from Nazi control. The invasion, known as D-day, remains one of the largest seaborne invasions in history.

provide ammunition and other supplies to the troops on the front line. On June 6, 1944, over 160,000 Allied soldiers crossed the English Channel and stormed the beaches of Normandy, where heavily armed German forces were waiting. The operation was called D-day; when the day was over, more than nine thousand men had been killed or wounded. Those who survived, including Patsy Giacchi, began the long, overland trek through France and into Germany to liberate Europe from Nazi domination.

On the last day of the war, Giacchi was sheltering in a foxhole in southern Germany when he and his comrades

Operation Overlord

Planning began in 1943. It would be one of the largest military operations in history. Hitler knew an invasion on his turf was coming. But he didn't know where or when it would happen. He and his commanders believed their secret codes were unbreakable. They used an encrypting device named Enigma to transmit classified information. It used over two hundred trillion possible letter combinations. The Germans had no idea that the Allies had already cracked the code and were sending out misinformation to see if the enemy was aware of Operation Overlord, the planned invasion of northwest Europe along France's Normandy coast. As the day of the assault approached, there was no evidence that the Germans knew what was coming or that Enigma's secret inner workings had been decoded.

Preparations for Operation Overlord began in 1943. The Allies transported and set up supplies and equipment in Great Britain, and then assembled and trained nearly 150,000 troops. That December, the Allies chose General Dwight D. Eisenhower to command the Allied Expeditionary Force, organized into a total of nine sea and airborne divisions. The invasion plan called for landing the entire force on five beaches along sixty miles of coastline.

D-day, the day of the invasion, was scheduled for June 4, 1944, but a sudden storm on the English Channel caused General Eisenhower to postpone the assault. On June 6, this epic confrontation began, and when it ended, more than four thousand Allied soldiers lay dead. But the defeat of Nazi Germany was finally in sight.

heard someone shouting over a loudspeaker, “The war has ended! The war has ended!” At first, the men couldn’t believe what they were hearing. But then, once the truth grabbed hold, they were beside themselves with jubilation and began firing their rifles, sometimes shooting each other by accident. The next morning, Giacchi and the rest of the men in his company lined up in formation, waiting for their officers to tell them what their fate would be. When Patsy heard his name called out, he stepped forward and got the news he’d been hoping to hear: “Private First Class Giacchi, you’re going home!”

American servicemen and women celebrate the end of World War II in Europe.

Cities in Ruin

For civilians in Europe, the war's end rarely meant a sudden return to the life they had enjoyed before the war. Six years of fighting not only left the continent in ruins, but it also left much of the population destitute, traumatized, and struggling to survive among shuttered factories, decimated farms, and cities and towns reduced to rubble. Severe shortages of food brought hunger and malnutrition to people already forced to survive on very limited government rations.

Jodoigne is a city in Belgium, where a young girl named Andree grew up. She and her family were already poor before the war began. In 1940, when the Germans began their occupation of her hometown, hunger became an ever-present threat to the residents of Jodoigne. German officials confiscated farm goods and farm animals to feed their troops, leaving the people to glean whatever they could from the fields. Bakers, without sufficient grain, resorted to using fillers to make loaves of bread. Each Belgian family was provided with one loaf each week. In Andree's family of four, one loaf had to feed them for seven days; it was never enough.

The family had one egg-laying hen, which became one of their most highly prized possessions. The hen laid only one egg each day, and Andree and her two sisters took turns each night eating the daily egg for dinner. Throughout those terrible years of hunger, their mother never once ate one of the eggs, choosing to starve herself than deprive her children of a bit of protein. Each night the hen was taken inside their house to prevent their neighbors from poaching it and turning it into a meal. And after the war, when the hen was too old to lay any eggs, Andree's family still cared for her. When she finally died in 1949, they gave her a funeral ceremony worthy of all she had given to them.

The never-ending search for sufficient protein forced Andree to rely on desperate schemes to satisfy her hunger. While some folks caught rats and consumed them, Andree much preferred songbirds. Each bird provided less than a spoonful of meat, but this was enough to supply Andree and her family with a much-needed source of protein. She devised an ingenious method for trapping the little creatures: First, she stretched a string across the garden behind their house; then, she coated the string with a sticky substance and sprinkled tempting crumbs and seeds on the grounds below. Drawn to the food, the birds would perch on the string and become stuck, unable to escape.

Looking back on those years, Andree regrets having to resort to what she sees as her cruel behavior. During and after the Second World War, famine ravaged much of Europe, taking the lives of over a million people. In countries under German occupation, the enemy's plundering of resources left the population facing life-threatening shortages of everything they needed to survive. The situation became so dire that people in East Prussia, a former German province, fell to eating dead dogs. In Naples, desperate people raided the city's aquarium and stole all the fish in order to have something to eat. In Berlin, children survived on grass from the city's parks. In Holland, sugar beets and tulip bulbs were a source of nutrition. Poor and working class mothers throughout Europe often turned to prostitution to put food on the table and keep their children from starving.

British and American troops who arrived in Europe after the liberation were expecting to witness catastrophic destruction. What they weren't prepared for was the degree of destitution among the surviving populace and their desperate scramble for even the slightest means of subsistence. Ray Hunting, a British army officer stationed in Italy in 1944, was shocked by the sight of hungry mobs of civilians crying out for food. Arriving by train, the officer felt he had to do something to help these people. So he tossed some of his ration tins out of an open window and into the nearby crowd.

As at least one historian has pointed out, food not only nourishes the body, but it also has a spiritual dimension. In that sense, it feeds the human spirit. When people are getting enough to eat and are in reasonably good health, they have more freedom to focus on other pursuits than constantly fearing starvation. Aid workers in postwar Europe, having direct contact with starving civilians, understood all too well how prolonged deprivation can destroy a person's humanity.

The War's End in America and Europe

Many people, growing up in the United States, are familiar with iconic images of the war's end and the celebrations that followed, at least in countries like America where the fighting had occurred overseas, thousands of miles away. One such image was published in *Life* magazine shortly after the Japanese surrendered on August 14, 1945. Victory Over Japan Day, or V-J Day, would officially be celebrated on September 2, 1945. The image is a photograph of a sailor bending over the woman in his arms and kissing her in Times Square, New York. Onlookers are smiling, perhaps even cheering on the young couple. (It turns out they weren't actually a couple; the sailor was with his date, a different woman, when he heard the news that the war in the Pacific was over. Rushing out to the streets from a movie theater, he grabbed someone he thought was a nurse and gave her the now-historic kiss.)

In Europe, despite the conclusion of the war, an atmosphere of mourning prevailed. Statistics alone hardly

Upon hearing that the Japanese had surrendered and the war in the Pacific was over, this excited United States sailor embraced a nurse in Times Square, New York. The couple did not know each other before this famous kiss.

do justice to the appalling loss of life, and the destruction of centuries of cultural development and of architectural marvels like grand cathedrals and palaces going back to the Middle Ages. Entire towns were leveled to the ground, leaving nothing behind but the skeletal ruins of what once were people's homes and the buildings where they had shopped and worked.

The war displaced millions of civilians, creating one of history's worst refugee crises. Many of the displaced were women and children taken captive by the enemy, along with traditional prisoners of war. In Germany, by the end of the war, an estimated eight million non-Germans lived like slaves, forced to work in factories and mines and on farms. When the war ended, these captive workers, finally liberated, took to the roads and highways, hoping to return to their homes and loved ones. Fierce bombing raids by the Allies drove millions of German citizens out of the cities; in Eastern Germany, millions more fled the advance of the Soviet Union's Red Army. In the last year of the war, there were nearly seventeen million people displaced just in Germany.

Unrelenting killing and destruction left European families torn apart and suffering the loss of at least one parent. Orphaned children roamed the continent in search of food, shelter, and safety. In Italy, one year after hostilities ceased, about 180,000 children had no place to go but doorways and alleys and no way to sustain themselves except by stealing, begging, and prostituting themselves. Over fifty thousand German children in occupied Berlin had lost their families and were wandering the streets, struggling to survive.

The Second World War left much of Europe and Asia in ruins and took the lives of around 4 percent of the world's population.

Rebuilding Europe

A major question facing the victors in the aftermath of the war was how best to manage the reconstruction of continental Europe. When the Big Three leaders of the Allied powers convened in Potsdam, Germany, this question underscored their deliberations concerning a variety of unresolved issues, including the future of a defeated Germany; the boundaries of Poland; the role of the Soviet Union in Eastern Europe; the amount of reparations Germany would be required to pay; and the ongoing war against Japan.

The conference in Potsdam was the third time since 1943 that the leaders of Great Britain, the United States, and the Soviet Union had met to iron out their differences and plan for an eventual peace between the Allies and the **Axis** powers, principally Germany, Italy, and Japan. By 1945, during the conference in this Berlin suburb, relations between the Big Three were anything but cordial. Since the previous gathering in Yalta several months earlier, United States president Franklin Delano Roosevelt had died due to a stroke and was replaced by his vice president Harry S. Truman, who was fiercely anti-Communist and had no experience in conducting foreign policy. Like Winston Churchill, Truman mistrusted the Soviet leader Joseph Stalin and was suspicious of his motives. Stalin's unwillingness to compromise on certain key issues, particularly the fate of Germany, only served to drag out the negotiations, which lasted for two weeks. According to historian Herbert Feis, the spirit of cooperation and camaraderie that had existed during the previous two conferences had all but dissipated. Now, Feis contends, the victors' thoughts "were brushed by the cold snow of mutual distrust and dislike."

At Yalta, the Allies had reached agreement on several points, including free elections in Eastern Europe, where the Soviet Union held sway. However, by the time of the Potsdam conference, the Red Army and the secret police had already eliminated the pro-democratic governments of Romania, Hungary, and Bulgaria in the east and put in place a Communist leadership. Furthermore, Stalin was unequivocally opposed to the interference of Western powers in Eastern Europe.

But despite their growing suspicions and distrust, the Allies understood that reconstruction was not simply a matter of rebuilding shattered buildings, clearing roads, reforesting the land, removing lethal mines, and reviving Europe's battered, broken-down industry and agriculture; for reconstruction to succeed, the political and economic systems of Europe had to be transformed in ways that would provide lasting benefits to the population and reduce the likelihood of another world war for generations to come. Only a strong foundation could serve as a guarantor of peace and an end to the competing and sometimes shortsighted policies of national governments. The leaders of the West, Truman and Churchill, had one vision of a postwar Europe; the Soviet leader, Joseph Stalin, had something quite different in mind. And this difference in outlook, based on history and conflicting interests and ideologies, can be seen as the source of mounting tensions and the basis of the Cold War.

The fragile state of societies in Western Europe left them vulnerable to pressure from armed minorities opposed to a capitalist economic system and in favor of a Communist-inspired revolution—one that would empower the poor and the working class and limit the influence of right-wing political parties. The Soviet Union's domination of Eastern Europe caused many officials in the Truman administration to sound the alarm, fearing that the Soviets would seek to expand their influence from east to west. Historians who study the early years of the Cold War hold differing views on the motives and actions of the major players, namely the United States and the Soviet Union. The standard view is that Soviet aggression was threatening freedom-loving people in

Europe. Only an iron-fisted response from the West would stem the tide of Communism and allow democracies to flourish. From this perspective, actions undertaken by the United States could invariably be understood as benign efforts to uphold the principles of self-determination, free elections, and democratic governance. Standing in the way, at least in the eyes of those who held the standard view, was an international Communist conspiracy whose headwaters was the Soviet Union (later called the "evil empire" by President Ronald Reagan in a speech he gave on March 8, 1983).

The Role of George Kennan

In 1946, George Kennan, a highly respected diplomat, State Department Russian specialist, and United States ambassador to the Soviet Union, sent a **long telegram** from Moscow to Washington in which he discussed Soviet intentions in Europe. Kennan argued that the Soviets were not content with consolidating their control over Eastern Europe; rather, they sought to take advantage of Western Europe's postwar disorder and instability by promoting and fomenting Communist revolution in targeted nations. To prevent this from happening, Kennan called upon the United States to follow a middle path between all-out war and appeasement (the willingness to concede to Soviet demands). America, he wrote, must undertake a "long-term, patient but firm and vigilant containment of Russian expansive tendencies." The strategy of **containment**, according to Kennan, should be based on "non-provocative resistance" rather than resorting to military force.

Dean Acheson

As secretary of state from 1949 to 1953, Acheson was instrumental in developing US foreign policy during the Cold War. When World War II ended, he became a committed anti-Communist who regarded the Soviet Union as a major threat that had to be confronted. During his tenure in the State Department, he played a leadership role in organizing the North Atlantic Treaty Organization (NATO), a peacetime alliance against the Soviet Union and its Communist allies. In addition to opposing the Soviet threat to Europe, NATO was also established to keep West Germany from becoming another Soviet satellite.

Acheson went to work turning Truman's ideas into what has become known as the Truman Doctrine. Initially, legislators in Washington were not convinced of the urgency of siding with the Greek government in their war with left-wing forces. But Acheson, during a briefing with members of Congress, described the Soviet Union as poised to expand its domain across Africa, the Middle East, and Europe.

In the same year, 1947, as undersecretary of state, he codeveloped the Marshall Plan, America's answer to the catastrophic devastation of Europe. Also in the 1940s, Dean Acheson took part in negotiations that produced several major global institutions: the United Nations Relief and Rehabilitation Administration, the International Monetary Fund, and the Food and Agriculture Organization.

A controversial figure with a caustic personality, Acheson focused mainly on Europe during his tenure in the State Department. However, he also became involved in a number of non-European Cold War issues, including the Korean War, negotiations to control the spread of atomic weapons, and the defeat of mainland China by Communist forces.

George Kennan's recommendations, particularly his advocacy of containment, formed the core of President Truman's approach toward the Soviet Union. In January 1947, Truman appointed George C. Marshall as his new Secretary of State. During the war, Marshall had served as the Army Chief of Staff and was regarded as perhaps the most important leader in the entire United States military establishment. Shortly after his appointment by Truman, a political crisis in Greece provided the first opportunity for the United States to respond to the threat of Communist subversion in postwar Europe. Marshall proposed giving financial aid to Greece as a way to avert the crisis and keep Communist insurgents from seizing power. His assistant, Dean Acheson, warned that the Greek crisis was evidence of Soviet infiltration into the affairs of another country. Unless the United States acted, he said, Soviet domination would continue to spread.

Following Germany's defeat, the country and its capital, Berlin, were divided into four sectors under Allied control. They remained divided throughout the Cold War.

CHAPTER TWO

The Marshall Plan and the Truman Doctrine

When the Soviet Union finally collapsed from internal as well as external causes, many people attributed its demise to our unyielding defense of freedom and democracy. The United States had succeeded in keeping the world out of the clutches of the Soviets and their pernicious ideology, which negates the value and intrinsic rights of the individual and substitutes a controlled economy for free market enterprise.

Another Look at the Cold War

But how accurately does this picture convey the actual conduct of the United States and the USSR during the Cold War? Though the war has ended, many questions remain. For example, to what extent did it allow both sides to pursue their separate agendas without undue interference or obstruction from the opposing side? Similarly, to what extent did the United States justify its own aggressive behavior on the basis of Cold War paranoia? On the one hand, the United States waged war against countries in the third world and supported repressive governments in the name of fighting Communism. The Soviet Union, for its part, permitted no dissent among its citizens and brutally repressed the countries it dominated in Eastern Europe, using fear of Western aggression and subversion to justify violence and repression within its own domains.

In 1950, Paul Nitze, a high-ranking government official, and his policy-planning staff produced one of the most influential documents of the Cold War. A fifty-eight page memorandum known as NSC-68 (National Security Council Paper 68), this top-secret document remained classified until 1975. It stated that the Soviet Union's "hostile design" posed a grave threat to the security of the United States and its allies.

By 1950, when NSC-68 was completed, the Soviet Union had already provided substantial evidence of its "hostile design": when World War II ended in 1945, the Soviet Union sought to create a buffer zone composed of countries along its western border. The main purpose for having such a zone was to prevent another invasion from the West such as the German invasion that had killed millions of Soviet citizens and soldiers.

Civil War in Greece

In February 1944, the head of the Soviet Union, Joseph Stalin, attended a conference in Yalta, a Russian resort town, along with Churchill and Roosevelt. The Allied leaders, looking forward to an imminent end to the war in Europe,

The President

~~TOP SECRET~~

NSC 68

COPY NO. 1

A REPORT

TO THE

NATIONAL SECURITY COUNCIL

by

THE EXECUTIVE SECRETARY

on

UNITED STATES OBJECTIVES AND PROGRAMS FOR NATIONAL SECURITY

DECLASSIFIED by authority of:
HENRY A. KISSINGER - ASST. TO THE
PRES. FOR NATL. SECURITY AFFAIRS
FEBRUARY 27, 1975
Signature H.C. Date 4-8-75

April 14, 1950

WASHINGTON

~~TOP SECRET~~

This is the first page of National Security Council Report 68 (NSC-68), a top-secret Cold War document completed in 1950 and not declassified until 1975. The report highlighted the threat to United States national security as a result of the Soviet Union's "hostile design."

planned how best to manage a postwar environment. Stalin agreed to allow free elections in all the lands his army had liberated from Nazi Germany. But once the war ended, he went back on his promise and made sure only Communist

Leaders of the Allied powers—British prime minister Winston Churchill, United States president Franklin D. Roosevelt, and Soviet premier Joseph Stalin—meet in the Russian town of Yalta in February 1945 to plan for the post-war world.

governments held power in the Eastern European countries of Albania, Bulgaria, Hungary, Czechoslovakia, Romania, Poland, and Yugoslavia.

Later that same year, in October, German forces occupying Greece began to retreat, fearing the advancing Red Army would prevent them from safely returning to Germany if they remained in Greece. By the end of the month, most of Greece was liberated from Nazi control. Although British troops had begun arriving earlier that month, the Greek resistance movement played a pivotal role in ending the occupation. Once the Germans were gone, the people celebrated, but their joy at being free was short-lived. Tensions between different resistance groups and between the resistance as a whole and the Greek government boiled over into a savage civil war.

With the Germans gone and Greece liberated, Great Britain organized a coalition government in Athens that brought together the two main resistance organizations: the Communist-dominated EAM–ELAS (National Liberation Front–National Popular Liberation Army) and the EDES (Greek Democratic National Army or National Republican Greek League), a group of right-wing National Army officers loyal to the king and his government-in-exile in Egypt. Members of EAM–ELAS wanted to build a radically different society, one that would be founded on the same principles that had inspired the Russian Revolution. By contrast, EDES members wanted the restoration of the Greek monarchy and a return to the status quo that existed before the war.

EAM representatives withdrew their support from the fledgling government when negotiations failed to resolve key issues. On December 3, 1944, fighting broke out in the capital between members of EAM and government forces, including security battalions formed under the previous government and mainly consisting of Nazi sympathizers trained to fight the Communist resistance. The conflict temporarily ended when British troops intervened, taking the side of anti-Communist organizations and those Greeks who had collaborated with the Nazis.

In March 1946, when a general election was held, the Communists abstained from voting, and two right-wing parties received the majority of votes. The new government cracked down on anyone with left-leaning or even liberal

Fearing the arrival of the Soviet army, German soldiers lower the Nazi flag over the Acropolis in Athens, Greece in the summer of 1944.

opinions. Communists as well as frightened citizens were forced to go into hiding in order to avoid persecution for opposing the government. Six months after the election, sixty-eight percent of the Greek people voted in a **plebiscite** for the return of the exiled king and the restoration of the monarchy.

By now, the civil war in Greece was more than Great Britain could manage. Its economy was straining under the burden of supporting the right-wing government in its campaign against the Communists. In 1947, Great Britain pulled its forces out of Greece, leaving room for the Americans to step in and finish the job of propping up the government. For many scholars and historians, the crisis in Greece represented the first battle of the Cold War and provided an opportunity for US president Harry Truman to engage more overtly with America's arch rival—the Soviet Union.

The Truman Doctrine

On March 12, 1947, President Truman addressed a joint session of Congress. His speech signaled the beginning of what has become known as the Truman Doctrine. The immediate impetus for the speech was the news that Great Britain would no longer provide economic and military assistance to the Greek government in its conflict with the Communists. Britain was also withdrawing its support of Turkey. Truman urged Congress to provide four hundred million dollars in emergency aid for both countries. He was less concerned with rebuilding Greece's shattered economy than about helping the government withstand a possible takeover by Communist forces, whom he believed were acting in concert with the Soviet Union. (Actually, Soviet leader Joseph Stalin did not get involved with the civil war and offered no aid to the Communists.)

Truman also feared that a Communist victory in Greece would destabilize neighboring Turkey and trigger waves of

British Complicity in the Greek Tragedy

In the autumn of 1944, after the Germans evacuated Greece, ending their brutal occupation, the group with the greatest amount of power and influence was the Communist-dominated resistance. When the British arrived a short time later, fifty thousand partisans—armed resistance fighters—agreed to serve under General Scobie, the British commanding officer.

On the morning of December 3, 1944, the British army opened fire on a group of Greek civilians in Athens. The civilians were expressing their support for the ELAS, the main component of the Greek resistance that had sided with the British in their fight against the Nazis. Only one day earlier, Communist representatives in the Greek government refused to sign a decree issued by the British ordering all members of the ELAS to disarm. The next day, hundreds of thousands of people took to the streets to protest the actions of the government and the British command.

But then the shooting began, and twenty-eight civilians were killed. Hundreds more were wounded. Their assailants included British snipers and Greek collaborators, who only weeks earlier had rounded up suspected members of the resistance, torturing and sometimes executing them. Why would the British attack the very people they had previously regarded as allies? Winston Churchill, the British prime minister, was aware of the Communist influence in the Greek resistance movement. But its growing strength was more than he anticipated; it threatened to overturn his plan to restore the exiled Greek king to power.

unrest in other parts of the Middle East, a region of great strategic importance to the United States. In addition to financial support, Truman also wanted Congress to authorize sending American civilian and military equipment and personnel to both Greece and Turkey.

The speech marked a dramatic shift in America's foreign policy, particularly in its relation with the Soviet Union. During peacetime, the United States historically refrained from getting involved with conflicts beyond the Western Hemisphere. But the postwar emergence of the Soviet Union as a superpower with ideologically opposed interests and

In his address to Congress on March 12, 1947, President Truman established what has become known as the Truman Doctrine, which played a significant role in United States foreign policy throughout the Cold War.

ideals compelled the United States to refashion its role in the world. Policy makers and political analysts in the government wanted to prevent the Soviets from expanding their influence. To that end, they advocated direct assistance to any nation under pressure from anti-democratic forces, especially when doing so was in America's best interests. The Second World War had clearly shown that our national security could no longer be separated from events taking place beyond our borders. Preserving our way of life and safeguarding our security would require strengthening our own economic and political systems as well as those of our allies.

The Truman Doctrine was the first step toward a far more comprehensive effort to contain the Soviet Union while helping Europe recover from the massive trauma and cataclysmic damage of the Second World War. That effort carries the name of its most influential proponent—George Marshall, US Army Chief of Staff during the war and Secretary of State in the Truman administration.

The Marshall Plan

Historians have tended to view the Marshall Plan as a singular, unprecedented event in the evolution of America's foreign policy. Originally called the European Recovery Program, the plan signaled the new, more forceful role the United States would henceforth play as a leader in the Cold War. The nation's traditional isolationist approach to world affairs was fast eroding.

A more recent and alternative view of the Marshall Plan places it squarely in the context of American history from

Truman Signs Aid Bill

Secretary of State George Marshall's June 5, 1947, address to Harvard's graduating class included a suggestion to European leaders. He recommended that they jointly develop a plan for economic recovery.

From this modest, informal beginning came the Marshall Plan, officially known as the **European Recovery Program**. Secretary Marshall may have "started the ball rolling" with his comments to Harvard graduates. But the work of turning his vision into an actual program took months of hard work and the dedication of numerous experts in various fields. Only a few weeks after his speech, the Foreign Ministers of France, Great Britain, and the Soviet Union met in Paris to discuss an economic rehabilitation plan, along the lines Marshall had suggested.

However, before any sort of agreement could be reached, Soviet Foreign Minister Vyacheslav Molotov found many aspects of the plan objectionable. Before walking out of the conference on July 2, he delivered a prepared statement in which he outlined his reasons for rejecting the proposed aid program. He felt that such a program would entail the creation of a central organization with powers "over and above the countries of Europe."

According to the *New York Times*, on April 3, 1948, after months of debate, "President Truman signed … the Foreign Assistance Act of 1948, which made the long-debated European Recovery Program an actuality. 'This measure,' he said, 'is America's answer to the challenge facing the free world.'"

the 1920s through the 1940s. From this perspective, the plan does not represent an unprecedented break from American diplomacy; rather, it is an extension of three decades of struggle to create a new economic order at home and overseas. The struggle began at the end of the First World War in 1918. The so-called New Era of the 1920s witnessed a significant reshaping of America's social and economic life. Trends begun during this period in our history continued into the 1930s when New Deal legislation enacted under President Roosevelt greatly increased the role of the federal government

In the 1930s, a severe economic crisis affected the United States and much of the industrialized world. Known as the Great Depression, it resulted in massive unemployment and poverty.

in regulating the economy and mitigating the hardships caused by the **Great Depression**. Traditionally, America had embraced a **laisser-faire** approach to the economic interests of individuals and to society as a whole. The principle of laisser-faire held that people should be allowed to pursue their interests without undue interference from the government. But from the 1920s onward, the rugged individualism of an earlier era was slowly giving way to a more managed, centrally regulated, and highly bureaucratic form of **capitalism**.

Challenges in Building an Economy

The growth of corporations, development of the country's industrial **infrastructure**, mass media, new technologies, and new ways of managing the economy in the 1920s and 1930s changed how America related to the rest of the world and the policies it pursued. Many influential people in both the private and public sectors wanted to remake the global economy in ways that would mirror and complement the changes taking place in the United States. In the 1940s, one of the greatest challenges facing the government was how to rebuild and restore the ravaged economies of Europe. After the First World War, America played a decisive role in helping to rebuild Europe. Now, decades later, in the aftermath of an even more disastrous conflict, officials in Washington searched for ways to promote economic growth and bring lasting peace and stability to Europe and hopefully the rest of the world.

Economists and leading politicians in the United States as well as in Europe believed that an integrated European economy should be the aim of any plan to rebuild Europe. Furthermore, they strongly advocated a **multilateral** system of world trade that would prevent, or at least impede, the overwhelming dominance of one national economy at the expense of the others. Planners involved in Europe's recovery effort couldn't always agree on the role Germany should play in the postwar world. France expected that its economy would provide the "engine of growth" driving recovery, while some officials in the Truman administration felt that this role should be filled by Germany, given its industrial capacity and access to major sources of energy, mainly the extensive coal fields found in the Ruhr Valley.

One principle that gained wide acceptance among many American planners was that the health and productivity of the American economy depended on trade and investment overseas. This, in turn, necessitated the restoration of important trading partners in Europe and their integration into a multilateral trading system. Americans clearly saw that Europe possessed an abundance of assets vital to America's economic interests. These assets included markets for American-made goods and agricultural products, a large workforce, technological knowledge, and advanced industry.

The end of the war had left a power vacuum in Central and Western Europe. One of the most formidable challenges facing the Truman administration was finding a way to prevent the Soviet Union from filling that vacuum and, in effect, gaining control of Europe's vast resources, which would pose a serious threat to American economic, political, and strategic concerns. The solution was fairly evident: create a **balance of power** in Europe by rebuilding the continent's political and economic systems. A strong, integrated Europe would provide the best shield against future Soviet aggression and the spread of Communism through indigenous political parties taking power in countries like Greece and Italy. A viable balance of power, besides offsetting Soviet advances, would also benefit the United States by maintaining our access to Europe's resources and our alliances with key trading partners. In the long run, the United States' own national security and standard of living were closely related, if not dependent upon, Europe's reconstruction and her secure placement within a global capitalist framework built to withstand the Communist threat.

Policymakers in Washington agreed that integrating Europe's varied and historically competing economies would help control German nationalism and balance Germany's recovery with France's entirely rational concerns about its own security. This integration would also reduce inequality, weaken class divisions and the dangerous tension these divisions produced, and create a balance of power in the West that would contain the USSR's growing power in the East. Before the Marshall Plan was proposed as the means to achieve the twin goals of European integration and economic recovery, other ideas were tried but with only limited success.

One concept that gained considerable traction was using America's economic and political systems as a model for rebuilding Europe. The size of our domestic economy and its management by central institutions had brought tremendous growth, social stability, and a high standard of living. Politically, our government was founded on the principle of federalism, in which power is not monopolized by one entity. In the United States, this means each citizen is subject to the laws of the city, county, and state in which he or she lives as well as the laws of the federal government in Washington, DC.

Policymakers in the Truman Administration thought it would be possible to create a "United States of Europe" in which the different countries would function much like our own states, and the economy as a whole would be centrally controlled and coordinated. At least, that was the dream. Making it happen was another matter entirely. By 1947, it was clear that previous attempts to stimulate Europe's recovery were failing. Part of the reason was the severe winter in 1946 and 1947, which exacerbated food shortages, held back manufacturing, and nearly destroyed previous economic advances. To make matters worse, people were earning less money and feeling hopeless after having lost so much because of the war. Social unrest, particularly in France and Italy, was threatening to topple established governments and leave the door open for Communist parties to win more adherents. In postwar Germany, divided by the Allies into four occupation zones, conditions were the worst. The country was supposed to have served as the engine that would pull Europe out of poverty and despair and toward full economic recovery. But the **level-of-industry** plan, adopted by the four occupying powers in 1946, was failing. If the plan had succeeded, it would have allowed Germany to rebuild its economy without posing a threat to its neighbors.

The Moscow Foreign Ministers Conference

In March 1947, the Allies attended a major conference in Moscow (the Moscow Foreign Ministers Conference) to evaluate conditions in Europe and to plot the best way forward in stimulating economic recovery. But the French and Americans were unable to resolve their differences over managing the deteriorating situation in Germany. The French would not agree to revising the level-of-industry plan to allow Germany to increase its industrial output unless France's security concerns were addressed. The Soviets were willing to compromise on some issues, but in the end, they sided with the French and thwarted American proposals for helping Europe recover from the war.

If nothing else, the conference revealed that America's limited, piecemeal approach wasn't working; something much more comprehensive and focused was needed. Whatever its ultimate form, a new approach would use economic integration as the means to achieve the desired goals of reconstruction and social stability and of the establishment of political institutions based on the principles of democracy and capitalism.

The goals may have been clear, but the way forward remained blocked, mainly due to a conflict between the State Department and the War Department. Officials in the State Department wanted a balanced recovery between Germany and the rest of Europe. They feared that a major revival of the German economy would enable Germany to once again dominate the continent and threaten its neighbors.

On the other hand, the War Department (since renamed the Department of Defense) argued that German industry should be the powerhouse of Europe's recovery, a position that the French and the Soviets didn't accept.

The Marshall Plan Emerges

In 1947, former US president Herbert Hoover undertook a fact-finding mission to Germany and Austria. The trip was commissioned by President Truman, who wanted Hoover to investigate the possible reasons behind Germany's slow recovery and propose ways to help both countries become less dependent on financial support from the United States. Following the trip, Hoover issued a report in which he stated that the first thing to be done was to revitalize German industry. To that end, the level-of-industry plan should be revised to remove limits on production. Furthermore, two major energy regions—the Ruhr Valley and the Rhineland—should remain as parts of Germany, and safeguards should be established to prevent Germany from embracing the sort of militarism that had precipitated the First and Second World Wars.

The War Department fully endorsed Hoover's recommendations, which provoked a serious debate within the Truman administration, since the Department of State was against the revival of the German economy at the expense of her neighbors. However, officials recognized that something had to be done and were willing to consider a new strategy that would resolve differences between the two federal institutions in Washington as well as between national governments in Europe. Furthermore, a new strategy, if successful, would unite the European economies in a larger framework designed to curtail any renewed German drive for dominance. It was from these considerations that the Marshall Plan emerged as the most comprehensive and ambitious effort to enable Europe to recover from the war.

George Kennan's Role in the Marshall Plan

Though named after George Marshall, Truman's Secretary of State, the plan's overall direction and guiding principles were based on recommendations formulated by George Kennan,

George Kennan, an American diplomat, played a leading role in shaping the goals and strategies of the Marshall Plan, a comprehensive aid program to help Europe recover from the Second World War.

a Foreign Affairs officer who had been stationed in Moscow. Kennan and his newly formed planning unit would have two weeks to complete their assignment and recommend the best ways to advance European recovery.

Kennan and his staff met their deadline. In their report, Kennan outlined the depressing realities that the people of Europe faced in the aftermath of the war, including widespread poverty and homelessness. There were also devalued national currencies due to inflation and industrial and agricultural infrastructure badly in need of repair or replacement. To strengthen Europe and reduce its vulnerability to Communist parties competing in local elections, Kennan strongly advocated collective action on the part of European nations. The United States would provide short-term aid and other forms of support, but the individual countries must assume joint responsibility for making a recovery program succeed. The program Kennan envisioned would be comprehensive in scope and serve as the means to achieve the long-term goal of European integration and unity within a supranational framework.

Moreover, Kennan supported lifting the ceiling on Germany's industrial production and including Germany in the recovery program. For Kennan, America's contribution to a massive recovery program would not only provide humanitarian aid (the United States gave over twelve billion dollars in economic support), but it would also contain the spread of Communism and at the same time benefit the American economy. An economically viable Europe would once again provide markets for American manufacturing and agricultural products.

As a five-star general, George C. Marshall served as army chief of staff during World War II. After the war, Marshall was nominated secretary of state. In 1947, he presented a program for rebuilding Europe that has become known as the Marshall Plan.

Despite an ongoing feud between the State Department and the War Department over the role Germany would play in Europe's overall recovery, leading policymakers in the Truman administration endorsed Kennan's strategy for rebuilding Europe. These leaders doubted that the Soviet

Herbert Hoover served as the thirty-first president of the United States from 1929 to 1933. Despite his well-deserved reputation as a great humanitarian, his policies during the years of the Great Depression failed to reverse the country's economic decline.

Union and the United States were likely to resolve their differences any time soon. They also wanted the United States, France, and Great Britain—three of the occupying powers of Germany—to integrate their occupation zones and make them part of a larger Western Europe economic and political bloc. Such a unified group of countries would serve as a counterweight to the Soviet sphere in Eastern Europe.

Lower-level officials in the State Department strongly disagreed with any plan that would divide Germany and the rest of Europe into competing areas. If this were to happen, these officials argued, it would be next to impossible for Eastern and Western Europe to restore healthy trade relations. Regional rivalry would also make future wars all the more likely.

In the end, Kennan's proposals for Europe won out and became the basis of the Marshall Plan, announced by George Marshall in a speech he gave at Harvard University on June 5, 1947. Critics of the plan allege that it was both a way to promote economic integration as much as a means to contain the Soviet Union and advance America's own interests. They also maintain that the plan ultimately prevented East and West Europe from achieving a lasting unity.

However differently historians and scholars judge the purposes and efficacy of the Marshall Plan, the words spoken by Secretary of State George Marshall during his Harvard address remain worthy of emulation: "Our policy is directed not against any country or doctrine but against hunger, poverty, desperation, and chaos."

On January 20, 1945, Harry S. Truman assumed the office of vice president of the United States. Eighty-two days later, President Franklin Roosevelt unexpectedly died from a cerebral hemorrhage, and Truman became the country's thirty-third president.

CHAPTER THREE

The Faces of the Cold War

This chapter introduces some of the individuals who played key roles in the early years of the Cold War. Their various positions allowed them to develop strategies, policies, and organizations to aid Europe in reestablishing its economy and infrastructure. These key players also helped develop the Marshall Plan, which was America's bold strategy for promoting Europe's recovery from the Second World War.

Harry S. Truman

While numerous officials in Washington made significant contributions along the way, it was President Harry S. Truman who initiated the process in his historic speech to the United States Congress in March 1947. His statement of principles that would later encompass the Truman Doctrine signaled a major turning point in America's foreign policy, in general, and more particularly, in relation to the Soviet Union. Truman called for economic and military aid for Greece and Turkey and pressed upon his colleagues in Congress that America was duty bound to enable people around the world to remain free of totalitarian governments.

In his speech, the President argued for resisting Communist ideology and its repression of democratic structures of power. His words were an explicit challenge to the Soviet Union, which he saw as threatening worldwide subversion and conquest. Before long, Truman backed up his words with actions that set the Cold War on a course it would follow for nearly half a century.

A familiar image of Truman is that of a plain-speaking farmer from a small town in Missouri who grew up to become president of the United States. But that's only a small part of the story. Harry Truman was born in 1884. His father was a farmer and a mule trader. After his father's death, he managed the family farm until America entered the First World War. At the age of thirty-three, Truman voluntarily enlisted in the Army and was sent to France, where he served as captain of an artillery unit. His courage and leadership won him the respect and loyalty of the soldiers under his command.

After the war, Truman and a friend from the Army went into business together. They opened a haberdashery, a shop that sells men's clothing. But the business failed due to declining economic conditions in the early 1920s. Truman began his political career shortly after by winning the election for county judge. His growing success as a politician as well as the support of the democratic establishment in Missouri prompted him to run for the United States Senate. He won the election and moved to Washington to serve as his state's junior senator.

During his second term as senator, Truman began to attract national attention, mainly because of his efforts to reduce fraud and waste in the United States military without endangering America's preparations for entering the war in Europe. Having won public approval and the respect of his colleagues, Truman was chosen as Franklin Roosevelt's running mate in the 1944 presidential election. Roosevelt defeated his Republican opponent and was elected for a third term in office. Truman was sworn into office as vice president on January 20, 1945, but his term only lasted eighty-two days. On April 12, President Roosevelt died from a cerebral hemorrhage. Truman, like most of the nation, was in shock. The day after he took the oath of office and became the new president, Truman told reporters he felt as if "the moon, the stars, and all the planets had fallen" on him.

Scholars have pointed out that Truman had no foreign policy experience when he assumed the presidency. However, he was an experienced politician and had successfully managed large, often unwieldy bureaucratic organizations during his tenure as senator. But was he capable of managing the country's transition from war to peace and of representing America's strategic interests and goals in negotiations with Allied leaders Joseph Stalin and Winston Churchill? The Big Three met in Potsdam, Germany after the war to decide Germany's future. By this time, the temporary alliance among Britain, America, and the Soviet Union was coming undone, creating strained relations among the leaders meeting in Potsdam not only over Germany's fate but Soviet repression in Eastern Europe.

As vice president, Truman had not been briefed about the Manhattan Project, America's top-secret program to develop an atomic weapon. It wasn't until after he became president that he learned about the project from Secretary of War Henry Stimson. Upon hearing of the new weapon's awesome power and its potential to tilt the balance of power firmly in America's favor, Truman authorized the continuation of the Manhattan Project. An interim committee was charged with deciding whether to use the bomb against Japan. In early June, Truman agreed with its recommendation to drop the bomb without warning.

During the conference at Potsdam in July, Truman informed Stalin that the United States possessed "a new weapon of unusual destructive force" without providing details. (Stalin had already uncovered information about the bomb through his espionage system.) Although Germany had surrendered, the Allies were still at war with Japan in the Pacific. On July 26, Truman, Churchill, and the president of the Republic of China called upon Japan to surrender unconditionally.

The subsequent dropping of two atomic bombs on the Japanese cities of Hiroshima (August 6) and Nagasaki (August 9) remains one of the most controversial decisions of Truman's presidency. Historians generally credit Truman with successfully guiding the United States through the early years of the Cold War (1945–1952); others fault him for exacerbating tensions between the United States and the Soviet Union. They contend that Truman's hardline policy

On the morning of August 6, 1945, the B-29 bomber known as the *Enola Gay* dropped the first atomic bomb ever used in warfare on the Japanese city of Hiroshima. The city was obliterated by the blast, and hundreds of thousands of civilians were killed.

toward the Soviet Union only served to deepen the divisions between East and West and prolong the Cold War.

During his second term as president, Truman devoted considerable attention to domestic issues. His Fair Deal included a number of far-reaching, forward-thinking proposals to benefit the majority of citizens, such as increased aid to public education, federal protection of civil rights, development of more public housing, and national health insurance. Although most of these proposals failed to garner sufficient congressional support, they decidedly influenced the direction of the Democratic Party for many years to come.

Little Boy and Fat Man

During the Potsdam Conference at the end of World War II, President Truman informed Soviet premier Joseph Stalin about a new weapon in the United States arsenal: "On July 24 I casually mentioned to Stalin that we had a new weapon of unusual destructive force. The Russian Premier showed no special interest. All he said was he was glad to hear it and hoped we would make 'good use of it against the Japanese.'"

A few weeks later, on August 6, 1945, an American B-29 bomber approached the Japanese city of Hiroshima. The bomb the plane was carrying also had a name: Little Boy. Between ninety thousand and one hundred sixty-six thousand people died within four months. Three days later, another B-29 with a different pilot dropped a second atomic bomb on the Japanese city of Nagasaki. Between forty thousand and seventy-five thousand people died immediately from the explosion of Fat Man, the bomb's second nickname.

Historians continue to debate the question of whether the United States was justified in deploying these awesome weapons. In his *Memoirs*, Truman expressed his certainty that the bomb should be used:

> "The final decision of where and when to use the atomic bomb was up to me. Let there be no mistake about it. I regarded the bomb as a military weapon and never had any doubt that it should be used. The top military advisers to the President recommended its use, and when I talked to Churchill he unhesitatingly told me that he favored the use of the atomic bomb if it might aid to end the war."

Generations of American students have learned that the atomic bombing of Japan shortened the war in the Pacific and prevented the deaths of United States soldiers. However, recent scholarship disputes these claims and offers a much different interpretation. Additionally, most top American military leaders saw no military justification for dropping the bombs.

Herbert C. Hoover

An extraordinary individual, Herbert Hoover was once called the "Napoleon of mercy" because of his total dedication to humanitarian work. Unfortunately, as America's thirty-first president, his previous achievements and his passionate concern for improving the lives of others weren't enough to secure his reputation; he left office, after one term, a defeated man reviled by many for having failed to pull America out of the Great Depression. In 1929, the stock market crashed. What followed was one of the darkest periods in American history as the economy went into a tailspin, causing massive unemployment and widespread poverty.

President Herbert Hoover began his presidency with many ideas for improving the lives of American citizens. However, his reluctance to have the federal government intervene more forcefully in the economy led to his defeat in the 1932 election.

During the Great Depression, which lasted from 1929 to the end of the 1930s, soup kitchens and breadlines set up by charitable organizations provided free meals to desperately poor citizens.

Instead of providing direct federal relief to the millions of jobless workers, President Hoover limited his response to giving loans to the states and creating public works programs. These efforts were insufficient to alleviate the “hard times” that gripped the nation. In 1932, while campaigning by train for a second term, Hoover was frequently pelted with rotten vegetables and heckled by people who blamed him for the country’s economic woes.

By the end of that election, Hoover had lost in forty-two out of forty-eight states and was succeeded by Franklin Delano Roosevelt. But Hoover's defeat did not spell the end of his public service. Over the next twelve years, he wrote numerous books and pursued his lifelong humanitarian interests. In 1947, at Truman's request, Hoover traveled to Europe to investigate the reasons for Germany and Austria's slow economic recovery. Providing relief for the populations of these former enemies was costing the United States about half a billion dollars annually even though the war had ended two years earlier. Hoover returned from his mission with a set of recommendations for how to make both countries more self-sufficient and less dependent on foreign aid. His report emphasized the importance of reviving Germany's industrial sector in order to drive continent-wide economic recovery. The State Department was against taking this direction since officials in the department were more in favor of a balanced recovery that didn't single out one nation over another.

However, in the War Department, people agreed that rebuilding German industry should be a number one priority of any aid program. Despite the ensuing conflict between the two departments, Hoover's report motivated policymakers on both sides to seek a new approach to rebuilding Europe.

Before beginning his career in politics, Hoover had made a fortune as a mining engineer and businessman. Born in Iowa, he was raised in a Quaker family, which likely influenced his later work as a humanitarian. In 1914, while living in London and helping American citizens return home, Hoover became dissatisfied with the direction his life was taking. Already a multimillionaire, he felt there was more to life than just making money and searched for a way to become more involved in public service. The opportunity came when World War I broke out in Europe following the assassination of Austria's Archduke Franz Ferdinand and his wife during a state visit to Serbia. In short order, the Austro-Hungarian Empire invaded Serbia, and Germany invaded Belgium. The British blockaded Belgium's harbors in order to deprive the Germans of supplies and force them to capitulate.

The plan failed. Between the blockade and the commandeering of food and other supplies by the occupying German army, the Belgian people faced the very real prospect of starvation. Hoover could not sit by and do nothing in response to this humanitarian emergency. As a measure of his values, Hoover organized the Committee for the Relief of Belgium (CRB), a major relief effort, which provided about one billion dollars in aid, distributed five million tons of food, and kept alive over nine million people in Belgium and northern France. It was this work that earned him the title "Napoleon of mercy." Hoover was so single-minded in his pursuit of securing funds for the CRB and feeding Belgium that people began to see him as a force of nature. President Woodrow Wilson's secretary of war, Newton Baker, had this to say about Hoover:

> *Terrible to the Germans, terrible to the British and French, terrible to most of his American associates, terrible because of his relentless and unconquerable determination to keep the Belgians from starving, he scolded, threatened, and out-bullied every human obstacle; changed the policies*

of nations; and thwarted the most resolute determinations of cabinets, governments, and military establishments. He squeezed money out of stones and gathered food from the deserts.

In 1917, President Wilson invited Hoover to serve as United States food administrator, primarily because of the work he had done in helping Belgium survive the war. In his new role in Wilson's administration, Hoover was responsible for allocating domestic food supplies to feed both Allied armies and the American people. After the war, he served as director of the American Relief Agency, a government agency tasked with responding to famine in Europe. His humanitarianism earned him the respect of both Democrats and Republicans, and in 1920, both political parties wanted him to run for president. Instead of becoming a candidate, he accepted an invitation from President Warren Harding to serve as secretary of commerce in Harding's administration.

Hoover may have ended his political career in defeat, but his achievements in the service of humanity cannot be overestimated. It may very well be the case that he saved more lives than any other person in history. Hoover's philanthropy and benevolence set a new standard for America's role in the world.

George C. Marshall

The Marshall Plan is named after George Marshall, army chief of staff during the Second World War and secretary of state from 1947 to 1949. (The army chief of staff is a four-star general and typically the highest-ranking officer on active duty in the United States Army.) In a speech he gave at Harvard University on June 5, 1947, Marshall presented his vision of America's role in rebuilding the European economy. The principles he articulated would later become known as the Marshall Plan (also called the European Recovery

As the army chief of staff during World War II, General George C. Marshall was responsible for building and organizing the largest army in history.

Program), which resulted in American contributions exceeding twelve billion dollars in economic, agricultural, and military aid toward Europe's recovery. In 1953, Marshall was awarded the Nobel Peace Prize for his inspired leadership in implementing the plan named after him.

As chief of staff, Marshall organized an army of over eight million servicemen and women in the war with Germany and other Axis powers. (His position was essentially administrative; he did not actually command troops in the field.) His skill in planning military operations on a worldwide scale prompted Prime Minister Winston Churchill to call him "the true organizer of victory."

Marshall's introduction to the life of a soldier began when he enrolled in the Virginia Military Institute, graduating in 1901 as senior first captain of the Corps of Cadets. Over the next three decades, he steadily rose in rank, becoming army chief of staff in 1939. He became a five-star general in 1944. His distinguished military career included serving during the First World War in France under General Pershing.

Marshall's upbringing in a devout Christian family gave him a set of convictions that shaped his character and stayed with him throughout his life. British historian Andrew Roberts described him this way:

> *Good-natured, charming, with fine manners, Marshall was nonetheless a tough man, and knew it. Though a soldier at heart, he believed in peace. In 1940, while petitioning a Senate appropriations subcommittee for more funds for the military, Marshall reminded the*

The Siege of Leningrad

"Operation Barbarossa" was the code name for Nazi Germany's invasion of the Soviet Union. The attack commenced on June 22, 1941. Three months later, German forces encircled Russia's second largest city of Leningrad (renamed St. Petersburg in 1991). Trapped within the confines of the city were approximately three million inhabitants. Hitler, the chancellor of Germany, was confident the city would surrender, expecting it to "drop like a leaf." His troops were under orders to maintain a blockade to prevent any kind of supplies from entering the city. Starvation was his weapon of choice. The Germans were so sure of victory, they even printed menus of the lavish feasts they would enjoy in the city's famed Astoria Hotel to celebrate their conquest.

But first, the city would have to surrender. That's where Nazi calculations went wrong. The people did not give up. They held out for nearly two and a half years, surviving on a few paltry slices of bread each day and anything else they could find, including rodents and even dirt. There was no heat during the winter, practically no food, no supplies, and no means to escape. People began dropping dead from the cold, the lack of food, and the monumental effort it took just to keep going. The famine that gripped the people of this city was one of the worst ever experienced by an industrialized nation.

In the midst of this suffering, the Russian spirit found an outlet in artistic expression. Dmitry Shostakovich, one of Russia's greatest composers, somehow managed to create the opening movements of his Seventh Symphony. On August 9, 1942, in an act of resistance, a starving orchestra performed this work before an audience of equally weakened listeners.

When Soviet troops finally broke the siege, over a million people had died. But the city had never surrendered, and those who survived will forever be remembered for their indomitable heroism.

legislators that those who have firsthand experience of war are profoundly aware of the value of peace:

"I am more of a pacifist than you think. I went through one war, and I do not want to see another. My idea, however, as to the sound basis for peace may differ from others. I saw it from the start, and I do not want to see it again. … I say this in all sincerity. I do not believe there is a group of people in the United States who are more unanimous in their earnest desire to avoid involvement in this ghastly war than the officers of the War Department."

After the war ended, Marshall resigned from the army and pursued a second career as a diplomat and statesman. During his years as army chief of staff, he honed his diplomatic skills by participating in the conferences in Yalta and Potsdam and similar events. In addition to serving as an ambassador to China, Marshall also served as secretary of state and secretary of defense. His leadership during the war and his contribution to the postwar recovery of Europe constitute an enduring legacy.

George Kennan

In the long history of the Cold War, the name of George Kennan is at the top of the list of influential policymakers. Diplomat, historian, writer, and intellectual, Kennan is best remembered as one of the founders of America's Cold War policies. His eight-thousand-word "long telegram," which he composed in 1946 and sent to Washington from his office

American diplomat George Kennan advocated a "containment policy" to end Soviet expansionism after World War II.

in Moscow, gave President Truman and the entire national security establishment a much-needed direction for dealing with the Russians when the war ended. It was Kennan who advised administration officials to pursue a policy of "containment" in regard to Soviet advances, and containment became the guiding principle for future presidents right up to Reagan's presidency in the 1980s.

Kennan lived to be 101 years old and spent a good part of his professional life living outside of America. According to his biographers, Kennan as a young man was somewhat solitary. He didn't make friends easily and often felt like an outcast. While attending Princeton University as an undergraduate, he had planned on going with friends to Yale in New Haven, Connecticut to watch the game between the two football teams. But his friends left town without him. When he got to Yale, he didn't have a ticket, so he missed the game and returned to Princeton the way he had left—alone.

Despite his unwavering loyalty to the country he served, Kennan was not particularly fond of the American way of life and often criticized the unseemly behavior of fellow citizens. He also held a very low opinion of democratic governments, including his own, and thought ordinary people should have less influence over public policy. Rather, he said, good governance should be in the hands of "elites," who have the experience and education to make sound decisions. Known for his sometime biting comments and analogies, he once compared democracy to "one of those prehistoric monsters with a body as long as this room and a brain the size of a pin."

In Kennan's disparaging view, democracies are slow to react to danger, and when they finally do, they attack with so much blind ferocity, they end up not only destroying their enemy but their own environment. To his sister Jeanette, he wrote, "I hate the rough and tumble of our political life ... I hate democracy; I hate the press ... I hate the 'peepul' [people]; I have become clearly un-American."

In a book he never finished writing, Kennan called for making voting the exclusive right of white males. And yet, despite his controversial views, he was highly respected by his peers in the United States Department of State. His understanding of Russian history and the contemporary workings of the Kremlin (the center of power in the Soviet Union) made him an invaluable ally in the Cold War struggle against Communism.

Kennan held a variety of diplomatic posts in Yugoslavia, Portugal, Germany, and the Soviet Union. Early in his career as a foreign service officer, the State Department gave him an opportunity to pursue graduate study in a foreign language of his choice. Kennan chose Russian, which he then mastered after enrolling in a university in Berlin. In 1933, after Roosevelt reopened diplomatic channels with the Soviet Union, the State Department sent Kennan to Moscow to help set up a new embassy. He wrote in his memoirs about a "mysterious affinity" he experienced while living in the Soviet Union, the only country he ever felt at home in despite his misgivings about its totalitarian government.

Kennan even wondered if he had lived in the Russian city of St. Petersburg in a previous lifetime. The Russia he so greatly admired was not the Russia of Stalin or the Bolsheviks; rather, it was the land of the great nineteenth century Russian writers like Tolstoy, Dostoevsky, and Chekhov. Kennan had no illusions about **Marxism** and Communist ideology, but he did see Joseph Stalin's reign as a continuation of Russia's historical preference for autocratic rulers. Stalin, he argued, was using Marxist philosophy as a pretext for doing what Russian leaders have always done—rule with an iron fist.

George Kennan had no illusions about Stalin's intentions in postwar Europe. He also had little patience with people in Washington who advocated self-determination for other countries and adherence to international laws. For Kennan, these were unrealistic goals with scant chance of succeeding given what he saw as the nature of governments as well as of people. Kennan advised officials in the Truman Administration to "get real" in terms of its relations with the Soviet Union. For Kennan, Soviet and American goals and values were clearly incompatible. In the aftermath of the Second World War, expecting to get reasonable concessions from Stalin was out of the question. Stalin would seek to impose the Soviet system on all the lands he controlled, and that is what would happen in Eastern Europe.

Kennan's long telegram and his subsequent article, "Sources of Soviet Conduct," published in *Foreign Affairs*, presented a compelling, persuasive account of his views regarding future relations between America and the Soviet in the context of the Cold War. One sentence, in particular, captures the overarching goal of American actions, including the disastrous war it waged in Vietnam, for the next four decades: "It is clear that the main element of any United States policy toward the Soviet Union must be that of long-term, patient but firm and vigilant containment of Russian expansive tendencies."

The Economic Cooperation Administration created this poster to promote the Marshall Plan in Europe.

CHAPTER FOUR

Negotiation and Innovation

When Secretary of State George Marshall spoke at Harvard's commencement ceremony on June 5, 1947, there was no plan in place to help Europe recover from the ravages of the Second World War. But in his speech, Secretary Marshall recognized the extent of the devastation that Europe had suffered. He identified many of the specific problems that were impeding a successful rebuilding of the European economy and noted the breakdown of the entire economic structure.

Marshall's Address at Harvard University

Marshall recognized the magnitude of Europe's requirements. These requirements surpassed Europe's ability to pay, so Europe needed help. Of all the countries in the world, only America was able to offer this degree of assistance. But in what manner would it be given? As loans to the governments of those countries in need of help? As contributions of goods shipped to European ports? Marshall did not offer a blueprint for how America would help Europe in the aftermath of war. Nor did he specify the exact terms that would cover an aid program.

However, he pointed out the direction the program must take to have any chance of succeeding and identified the role the United States might play:

> *The role of this country should consist of friendly aid in the drafting of a European program and of later support of such a program so far as it may be practical for us to do so. The program should be a joint one, agreed to by a number, if not all European nations.*

The United States would not be doling out vast sums of money or goods to needy governments in Europe. On the contrary, it would be up to the Europeans themselves to craft a program of aid. Moreover, the nations of Europe would have to put set aside their differences and work together to decide what they needed and how they might expect to pay for whatever goods and services they received as part of the program.

Months of deliberations and negotiations on both sides of the Atlantic followed Marshall's address at Harvard, which the British Foreign Secretary Ernest Bevin called "one of the greatest speeches in world history." It was this speech that proposed the goals and objectives of what would subsequently become the Marshall Plan, a program that provided over twelve billion dollars in aid to eighteen Western European countries. The program did not blossom

On April 3, 1948, President Truman signed the Economic Cooperation Act, which authorized the Marshall Plan for Europe's recovery.

into being overnight. On the American side, it took nearly a year from the time of Marshall's speech to passage of the **Economic Cooperation Act (ECA)**, signed into law by President Truman on April 3, 1948. The law established the European Recovery Program, the official title of the Marshall Plan.

For the Marshall Plan to work, European governments would need to cooperate and, as far as possible, integrate their economies within a decidedly capitalist framework. Figuring out how to do this was the task facing the numerous committees meeting in European capitals as the Marshall Plan began to take shape. What separated this plan from other aid programs was the degree to which the Europeans were primarily responsible for their own recovery. Instead of treating them like passive recipients of charity, the plan's visionary authors aimed to empower them by setting up a framework within which the Europeans would be in control of the recovery process, with nominal outside assistance.

The Conference on European Economic Cooperation

Only two weeks after Marshall gave his speech, French and British foreign ministers organized the Conference on European Economic Cooperation (CEEC) in Paris. The fourteen government representatives who attended the conference met from the end of June through September to draft a report on how much economic aid their countries needed. For many, the challenge of working jointly was a novel experience. Perhaps an even greater challenge was assessing their nations' economic needs in relation to the European continent.

Among the attendees was a large Soviet delegation led by Vyacheslav Molotov, the Kremlin's foreign minister. The Soviet delegates wanted no part of a plan that treated the entire continent, including Germany, as an integrated economic entity. From their perspective, the Marshall Plan was a blatant attempt by the United States to yoke all of Europe, including the Soviet Union's satellite states in the East, to the capitalist model of economic development. Their

Following George Marshall's proposal for a massive aid program, delegates from European nations attended the Conference on European Economic Cooperation (CEEC) held in Paris in the summer of 1947.

preference was to have each country independently inform the United States of what it needed. Then, the United States would simply package the requested goods and ship them over to Europe. But that was not how the plan was meant to work.

To Joseph Stalin, the Soviet premier, an integrated European market in which the production and distribution of goods and services, as well as of information, were not under strict government supervision was incompatible with the kind of political and economic system he was determined to impose in the East. When Molotov, his foreign secretary, realized he wasn't going to get his way at the Paris conference, he and his fellow delegates walked out. The Soviets' rejection of the Marshall Plan further damaged the already strained relations among the former wartime Allies. Not only did the Soviet Union refuse to take part in the Marshall Plan, but it also blocked the Eastern European countries from receiving any kind of aid.

In Paris, the other delegates, meanwhile, were beginning to realize what George Marshall meant when he proposed "a cure rather than a palliative." For the "cure" to take effect, Europe would need to undergo a deep, structural realignment of its separate economies (something that had never happened before).

The Organization for European Economic Cooperation

Rising to the challenge, the CEEC transformed itself into the Organization for European Economic Cooperation (OEEC), under the leadership of Paul-Henri Spaak, the Belgian foreign minister. Members of the OEEC did not always see eye to eye on the subject of aid—in particular, how much and to which country for what purposes. So making compromises was crucial, especially since no decision could go forward unless it was supported by every member.

At the time of the Marshall Plan, America was the leading economic power in the world. As such, it would have been tempting for those in charge of implementing the plan to force Europeans to accept certain ideological trappings or make their governments conform to America's desires. But that never happened. However, the United States did have an agenda: it wanted European economies to develop in ways that were much more open and much less

The Invention of the Transistor

Electronic devices need some sort of mechanism whereby a weak electronic signal can control a much stronger signal. Prior to 1947, the controlling mechanism used in electrical circuits was the vacuum tube. But vacuum tubes were large and used up a great deal of energy. As a result, the tubes generated heat, which shortened their lifespan. Large computers in the late 1940s used over ten thousand vacuum tubes.

The transistor proved to be much more efficient, requiring less electrical power and producing much less heat. It is among the most important inventions of the twentieth century. The first successful demonstration of a transistor occurred on December 23, 1947, at Bell Laboratories in New Jersey. The inventors were William Shockley, John Bardeen, and Walter Brattain. Shockley was a physicist. He had succeeded in working out the physics behind a transistor, but he had been unable to actually make one. So he called upon the talents of two fellow scientists—Bardeen and Brattain. It took them another two years to turn Shockley's theory into a working model. The transistor they developed was called a "point-contact" transistor. But it proved to be inferior to Shockley's improvement, which is called a "bipolar" transistor.

Thanks to the small size and efficiency of transistors, the field of electronics was dramatically transformed. Transistors made it possible to miniaturize the complex circuitry that operates computers. In the 1960s and 1970s, integrated circuits embedded on thin wafers of semi-conducting material replaced individual transistors.

regulated than Soviet-dominated economies. More to the point, the United States had no intention of allowing the West to slip into the Soviet orbit where Communism was the prevailing ideology. And, as mentioned earlier in this book, the United States had its own self-interests at stake. It needed a revitalized European economy as a market for American products. Reestablishing fruitful trade relations would serve to keep the American economy in tiptop shape while also benefitting Europe.

The Economic Cooperation Act

A key difference in the American approach to foreign aid was that countries in Western Europe were free to develop at their own pace and in a manner consistent with their unique political and social cultures. As part of the implementation process, the Economic Cooperation Act (ECA) of 1948 authorized the establishment of diplomatic missions in each country receiving aid. And each of these missions, in turn, was headed by a prominent political figure with sufficient stature to meet with high-level dignitaries in the governments of those countries.

Additionally, United States embassies in each of the member countries began negotiating mutual agreements with their host governments. These bilateral pacts stipulated the responsibilities of the governments toward their American sponsor. One such responsibility was to recognize the authority of the ECA mission set up in the capital. A formal committee served as the liaison between the mission and the government. Its most important task was to plan how to invest the money in the "counterpart fund."

Goods shipped from America to Europe under the Marshall Plan—like these bags of sugar—had to show where they came from. The original label approved by Congress was "For European Recovery—Supplied by the United States of America."

This fund was one of the distinguishing characteristics of the Marshall Plan. While some Europeans initially anticipated receiving liquid assets in the form of cash allotments or assets readily converted to cash, that was not how the plan operated. Instead of cash or similar assets, the United States shipped goods to Europe. The goods in turn were purchased by the receiving government using their own currency since they didn't have enough dollars to cover the costs. The money they paid was deposited in the counterpart fund, and this money was then used for national reconstruction projects according to prior agreements between the ECA mission and the participating government. Currency in the fund was typically used to rebuild civilian infrastructure damaged during the war, including schools, hospitals, bridges, roads, and airports. Among the many kinds of goods that the United States shipped to Europe were coal, wheat, corn, iron, steel, lumber, food, machinery, tractors, and fertilizer.

Once the process of implementing the Marshall Plan began, the program inevitably evolved, influenced by the cultural, political, and economic institutions and traditions of the various countries. The governments badly needed financial aid, but they also wanted to negotiate their own terms for dealing with their American benefactors. For example, the British were opposed to integrating their economy with the whole of Europe. The Austrians resisted America's proposals for reforming their railway and banking systems. The Greeks did not want to use a new form of currency; they preferred gold sovereigns as the only solid basis of financial transactions. A leading Italian industrialist informed the head of the mission in Rome that women in his country would never accept clothes made of cheap synthetic materials. They would only wear homemade clothing that used natural materials.

The Marshall Plan and Diplomacy

The process of developing and administering the Marshall Plan required substantial diplomacy on three basic levels: between the United States and Europe, among the nations of Western Europe, and between Americans and the people of Western Europe. Overall, the Marshall Plan was an expression of the United States's decision to provide humanitarian aid to Europe in order to help its people recover

In 1955, the original Marshall Plan label was changed to "Strength for the Free World—From the United States of America," reflecting growing efforts to promote the benefits of capitalism in response to the spread of Communism.

from the war and to enable the governments to remain free of Communist control. Nation-to-nation diplomacy required disparate governments to sit down at the negotiating table and work out their differences. For the most part, these countries lacked the sort of traditions and institutions that supported cooperation on the basis of shared goals. It would take several more decades of hard work before the European Union (created by the terms of the Maastricht Treaty in 1993) could become a reality.

One of the more innovative features of the Marshall Plan was its inclusion of Germany. Policy makers in the United States government wanted to avoid at all costs the mistakes that were made at the end of the First World War. In 1919, the victorious Allies—France, Great Britain, Russia, and America—drafted the Treaty of Versailles without any input from defeated Germany. Many historians agree that the harsh terms of the treaty contributed to the resurgence of German militarism and the start of a new world war.

Another innovation the Marshall Plan introduced to a foreign aid program was the United States Productivity Plan. While the transfer of technology and state-of-the-art machinery and industrial equipment was important to Europe's recovery, the Productivity Plan invited business

Productivity Missions

As part of the Productivity Plan set up under the Marshall Plan, European workers could apply for participation in a productivity mission to the United States. These missions gave workers an opportunity to learn about the latest management styles and technological innovations by attending training programs and seminars and visiting American companies.

Between 1949 and 1955, French industries sent multiple productivity missions to the states. A number of these industries were interested in knowing about new welding techniques. These techniques were important to industries involved in metallurgy and the manufacture of products using metal. The United States, at that time, was regarded as a world-class leader in the use of welding, which it had refined during the war through the production of ships, planes, and other types of transport vehicles.

In the fall of 1951, the French organized a welding mission that was sponsored by various associations. It was France's 118th productivity mission since 1948. The thirteen members of the welding mission came from trade and professional organizations, and all of them were engineers.

From October 11, 1951 to November 20, 1951, the team visited thirty-one sites in the north and northeastern regions of the United States, focusing on aviation, automotive, and construction industries. Thanks to this productivity mission, the French were able to transfer a range of new welding technologies from the United States to France and to adapt their own methods to techniques they studied in America. In addition, the mission showed them how a more efficient workshop organization could benefit overall production.

managers to participate in training programs in the United States. These programs, which ran for two or three months, taught modern management skills to participants. Besides attending training sessions, they traveled to US companies to see how American managers did their job.

The European Recovery Plan Information Program

To convince ordinary European citizens of the benefits of the Marshall Plan as well as to offset negative messages about the plan emanating from the Soviet Union, American planners launched the ERP Information Program. (ERP as in European Recovery Plan, the official title of the Marshall Plan.) It was one of the largest and most effective propaganda efforts ever developed by one country attempting to influence the opinions and choices of other countries.

The Information Program employed journalists, filmmakers, and writers to produce a wealth of documentary films, posters, pamphlets, radio programs, and traveling exhibitions. In addition to generating multimedia messaging, the program set up "productivity villages" in which European leaders could view model factories and workers' communities, and come away with a positive opinion of the free-market system. The various types of propaganda were tailored to different groups in each country. For example, workers and managers in industry learned of the benefits of scientific management, increased productivity, and an integrated European economy. For families, the Information Program promised better jobs, a better standard of living, and lasting security in Europe.

Due to the success of the Marshall Plan, Europe overcame the devastation and poverty that were the consequences of the Second World War.

CHAPTER FIVE

The Legacy of the Marshall Plan and the Truman Doctrine

Faber-Castell is a family-owned, pencil-making factory in Stein, Germany. The company has been in business since 1761. During the Second World War, the Germans used it to make munitions. By the end of the war, the original machinery remained in place, but the owners were not able to resume the production of pencils since they lacked sufficient currency to pay for supplies. The Nazi currency, the Reichsmark, was rapidly falling in value. Then came the Marshall Plan, otherwise known as the European Recovery Program. Because Germany had been included in the plan, a new currency, the deutsche mark, was issued with the backing of the American dollar. Thanks to the infusion of financial support, Faber-Castell went back into production. A favorable exchange rate between the German mark and the American dollar meant the company could now afford to import cedar wood, a high-quality material used to make the bodies of the pencils, from Stockton, California.

Faber-Castell

Ludwig Lihl began working at Faber-Castell in 1950. During an interview with a *Washington Post* journalist in the 1990s, he had a simple explanation for why his company could resume operations: "It would not have been possible," he said, "without the Marshall Plan." Brand-new Faber-Castell pencils, fresh off the assembly line, were delivered to newly reconstructed ports on restored roads and then shipped to destinations around the world. The wheels of commerce were once again turning in Germany, as well as in the rest of Western Europe, thanks in no small measure to the Marshall Plan.

The generous amount of aid provided by the plan enabled numerous small businesses, entrepreneurs, and farmers in Europe to put their lives back together. The plan's benefits weren't limited to small enterprises; it also financed the creation or restarting of some of the biggest, most profitable corporations in Europe, including such car manufacturers as Renault, Pechiney and Dassault in France, Volkswagen and Daimler-Benz in Germany, and Fiat in Italy.

The Impact of the Marshall Plan on Europeans

For ordinary Europeans, the plan meant the return of basic commodities unavailable or too expensive to purchase during the war. A former interior minister of France, when asked what the Marshall Plan had meant to him, answered, "white bread." For other people, it meant the end of ration cards,

Marshall Plan aid allowed European industry to resume full-scale operations.

the welcome return of eggs and butter to the markets, or the possession of enough money to buy a new winter coat. Germans who had been children during the years of the Marshall Plan recalled their first taste of canned American food. British citizens remembered having American orange juice once the plan came into effect. In Greece, the plan provided baby chicks to homemakers. The chicks, once mature, would provide eggs, a source of protein, for the homemakers and their families.

In Austria's mountainous resort areas, the plan meant ski lifts could be rebuilt. In Rotterdam, an important port city in the Netherlands, Marshall Plan aid allowed the city to purchase cranes, which were then used to rebuild the port that was badly damaged during the war. The plan operated for four years, from 1948 to 1952. During that brief amount of time, industrial production in Europe increased by thirty-six percent. Historians are reluctant to attribute this growth solely to the Marshall Plan, since Europeans themselves invested very large sums into their own recovery. But the plan, even though it represented only a fraction of Europe's total investment, more than likely accelerated the rate of growth in the view of many scholars.

European Industry

The plan also contributed to the reshaping of European industry. Two world wars had severely impacted the continent's industrial sector. In most of the countries in Europe, workers were highly trained and educated, but the machines and equipment they used were antiquated or badly in need of repair or replacement. To boost the level of productivity in European factories, the OEEC—founded in 1948 to manage American aid under the Marshall Plan—organized "productivity missions" to the United States. These missions consisted of white-collar workers (twenty percent), engineers or foremen (forty percent), and workers (forty percent). The training they received in America introduced them to the latest management methods and techniques for streamlining and modernizing their own production

This map shows European nations helped by the Marshall Plan.

facilities. The training also provided workers at all levels with firsthand exposure to the sort of consumer society that existed in the United States. The General Electric company in Philadelphia hosted initial productivity missions.

Another enduring legacy of the Marshall Plan was an innovative financial mechanism that allowed European nations to exchange their currencies with few of the restraints and limitations that had been in place before and immediately after the war. Before the euro became the single currency of nineteen of the European Union's member states in 1999, each country had its own currency (for example, Italy's lira, France's franc, and Greece's drachma). When the war ended, countries negotiated bilateral payment agreements based on exchange-rate controls. But when this method proved unwieldy and failed to adequately stimulate international trade, the OEEC decided in July 1950 to introduce a multilateral payment system. Two months later, the OEEC created a European Payments Union (EPU) to administer currency conversion based on exchange rates that reflected the economic status of each participating country. As a result of this switch to a new exchange mechanism and the loosening of restrictions on trade policies, inter-European trade noticeably improved. In turn, Western Europe moved one step closer to the kind of integration envisioned by George Kennan and his colleagues in the US State Department.

In addition to its impact on European industry, the Marshall Plan dramatically affected the culture of Western Europe. As standards of living improved with the influx of aid and the resulting rebirth of productivity, a new middle class emerged with a penchant for all things American, including American music and popular fiction, and American food. Young people, charmed by America's mass media, began preferring Coca-Cola to local beverages, reading paperback books, and listening to the latest records from America. The pervasive influence of American society—made possible by the Marshall Plan—challenged traditional European values and traditions. Many Europeans felt threatened by America's growing presence and worried they might lose their unique national and cultural identities in the modernization project underway.

The European Union

Nevertheless, the Marshall Plan laid the foundation for an integrated Europe. For many historians, the plan began a process that culminated in the creation of the European Union (EU) with the signing of the Maastricht Treaty in Maastricht, a city in the Netherlands. Leaders of the European Community of nations signed the treaty in 1992. It entered into force in 1993 and guaranteed citizenship of the European Union to every person who was a citizen in any one of the member states. The treaty also created a central banking system and a single currency (the euro), and called upon EU members to coordinate their foreign policies for the peace and security of the continent as a whole. Furthermore, EU citizens, regardless of nationality, can vote or run for political office in the EU country in which they live. Visitors to today's fully modernized Europe can expect to see some of

On March 25, 1957, representatives of six European countries signed the Treaty of Rome in Rome, Italy. This agreement established the European Economic Community in which a common market and the gradual elimination of tariffs would lead eventually to closer political and economic integration.

the more dramatic consequences of the Marshall Plan in the form of a high-tech railway system, beautifully restored cities, and markets displaying every conceivable consumer good.

The EU began as an association limited to the countries of Western Europe. But in the twenty-first century, it opened membership to countries in Central and Eastern Europe. Its current twenty-eight members include Croatia, Bulgaria, Poland, Czech Republic, Slovenia, Romania, Latvia, and Estonia.

The European Economic Community

Between the founding of the European Union and the implementation of the Marshall Plan, European nations instituted the European Economic Community (EEC), also known as the Common Market, with the signing of the Treaty of Rome in 1957. Originally six countries signed the treaty, which intended to integrate European economies. Six more countries joined by 1986, and East Germany became a member in 1990, after the fall of the Soviet Union and the reunification of Germany. The EEC removed most trade barriers among member states and established a single trade policy with countries not part of the EEC. By 1968, this community of nations succeeded in eliminating all internal tariffs, a significant obstacle to intra-European trade.

The EEC, like its successor the EU, is the direct descendant of the Marshall Plan, which provided the impetus and the inspiration for what is possible when people and their elected leaders work together to solve common problems. Because of its success in helping Europe recover from history's most destructive war, the Marshall Plan remains a source of guidance for addressing twenty-first century problems.

The Significance of the Marshall Plan and the Truman Doctrine

The Marshall Plan and the Truman Doctrine are often cited by scholars as two of the most influential Cold War policies enacted by the administration of President Harry Truman. When the Soviet Union purposely rejected the Marshall Plan and prevented its satellite states in Eastern Europe from participating, the **Iron Curtain** began to descend across the continent, creating a solid division between the East and the West. The seemingly irreconcilable differences between these two competing spheres fueled the Cold War, which lasted until the collapse of the Soviet Union.

When Truman spoke to Congress in response to the civil war engulfing Greece in the 1940s, he signaled a new direction in America's foreign policy—away from the country's traditional isolationism and toward a committed engagement with the rest of the world. The Truman Doctrine, as it became known, would use substantial economic aid to rebuild parts of the world damaged by war. In his speech, Truman requested an aid package of around four hundred million dollars for both Greece and Turkey. Fearing a Communist takeover, mainly in Greece, Congress approved the president's request. By alleviating the poverty and misery of the Greek people, the Communist message would have less appeal. At least, that was the expectation and underlying purpose of Truman's policy.

The Truman Doctrine introduced economic aid as a major element in United States foreign policy. Not only would aid revitalize impoverished regions, it would also promote

United States political goals. Subsequent administrations have followed in President Truman's footsteps, administering economic aid to parts of the globe where war and/or natural disasters have caused displacement and suffering. Under President John F. Kennedy, Congress passed the Foreign Assistance Act in 1961. The purpose of the Act was the following:

> *To promote the foreign policy, security, and general welfare of the United States by assisting peoples of the world in their efforts toward economic development and internal and external security, and for other purposes.*

In 1989, with the dissolution of the Soviet Union and the liberation of the countries of Central and Eastern Europe from Soviet domination, Congress passed the Supporting Eastern European Democracy Act (SEED):

> *The primary goal of [this Act] is to promote democratic and free market transitions in the former communist countries of Central and Eastern Europe, enabling them to overcome their past and become reliable, productive members of the Euro-Atlantic community of Western democracies.*
>
> *In 2010, a massive earthquake took the lives of hundreds of thousands of Haitians. In addition to relief efforts by international aid organizations, "President Obama pledged a swift, coordinated, and aggressive effort in response to the earthquake in Haiti in January and called for sustained commitment to Haiti's reconstruction.*

In the twenty-first century, the United States continues to apply the lessons learned in the 1940s when President Truman launched the Truman Doctrine, using economic revitalization as a key component of its foreign policy, especially in regard to American and Soviet relations during the Cold War. George Kennan, one of the architects of the Marshall Plan during Truman's Administration, once commented that "It is not Russian military power which is threatening us; it is Russian political power." Even President Eisenhower, who succeeded Truman in 1953, did not believe that the Russians ever intended to attempt a military conquest of Western Europe. If that was the case, then how do historians and political analysts explain the four-decades-long Cold War?

One plausible explanation is that it was a "system of global management" that permitted both sides to pursue their separate and often mutually antagonistic agendas without becoming a "hot war." While the Soviets kept an iron grip on their own domain in the East, the United States engaged in wars against third world countries. Both sides used fear of the other to control their respective citizenry and to justify ever-increasing military expenditures. When the Soviet Union and its tyrannical government finally dissolved and the Cold War ended, the United States had the upper hand in global affairs.

"Operation Just Cause"

On the morning of December 20, 1989, with the Soviet Union no longer a powerful deterrent, the United States

Bizonia and the Berlin Airlift

With the end of World War II, the alliance that had defeated Nazi Germany was beginning to crumble. A major source of contention was over the fate of Berlin. Conditions were abysmal for the people who resided in the city. As a result of Allied bombing raids during the war, most of the buildings had been reduced to rubble, starvation was a constant threat, and adequate shelter was practically nonexistent.

In the growing conflict between East and West, Berlin was becoming a powder keg where one wrong move might ignite World War III. On January 1, 1947, Great Britain and the United States combined their occupation zones in Germany to form "Bizonia." This move exacerbated tensions with the Soviet Union. Then came the announcement of the Truman Doctrine and the Marshall Plan, which hardened the divisions between East and West. That same year, occupation policies in Germany underwent radical changes as each side sought to gain the upper hand.

In 1948, the United States and Great Britain introduced a new currency into Bizonia and West Berlin in an effort to gain control of East Berlin's economy, among other goals. The Soviets retaliated with a currency of their own and a total blockade that kept out all essential supplies from entering West Berlin. The only way open to delivering aid was by air. On June 26, 1948, the United States began "Operation Vittles" followed by Britain's "Operation Plainfare." The airlift delivered over two million tons of supplies and involved 270,000 flights.

On May 12, the Soviets finally lifted the blockade. The Berlin crisis had been resolved without the superpowers turning the conflict into another war.

invaded Panama in "Operation Just Cause." The attack was authorized by President George H.W. Bush in order to arrest Panama's leader Manuel Noriega for drug trafficking. In 1990, when Daniel Ortega, a Cold War "enemy," was poised to win the national elections taking place in Nicaragua, the United States intervened, using economic pressure, among other strategies, to compel voters to elect someone more aligned with America's interests.

Instead of the "peace dividend" many people expected when the Cold War passed into history, the United States has embarked on a series of military adventures, mainly in the Middle East and parts of Africa. The world continues to be a place of great turmoil and misfortune that only a truly global Marshall Plan might have the power to assuage if not remedy. Helmut Schmidt, the former chancellor of Germany, had nothing but praise for the original Marshall Plan: "The United States ought not to forget that the emerging European Union is one of its own greatest achievements: It would never have happened without the Marshall Plan."

Chronology

1917 Year of the Russian Revolution, which actually involved two revolts: the first, in February, overthrew the Russian imperial government; the second, in October, brought the Bolsheviks into power.

1918 Western forces invade Russia; for some historians, the invasion marks the true beginning of the Cold War.

1919 The Allies, who defeated Germany in World War II, draft the Treaty of Versailles, which imposes very harsh terms on the Germans.

1922 The Soviet Union (Union of Soviet Socialist Republics) is formed.

1929 The stock market crashes; the Great Depression affects economies around the world.

1939 Germany invades Poland; the Second World War has begun. Germany and the Soviet Union sign a nonaggression pact.

1941 The United States enters the war.

1944 German troops begin to evacuate Greece, fearing the Soviet army will prevent them from returning to Germany. British troops in Greece side with right-wing forces in their conflict with Communist groups.

1945 The United States drops two atomic bombs on two different Japanese cities: Hiroshima and Nagasaki. The Soviet Red Army defeats the German army, which formally surrenders in Berlin to the Soviets. The war in Europe ends. Roosevelt is elected to a third term in office as president, with Truman as his vice president. On April 12, Roosevelt dies from a cerebral hemorrhage, and Truman becomes the new president.

1946 American diplomat George Kennan sends his "long telegram" to the US Department of State.

1947 Secretary of State George Marshall delivers the commencement address to Harvard University graduates.

1948 President Truman signs the Economic Cooperation Act, which establishes the European Recovery Program (otherwise known as the Marshall Plan). Representatives of fourteen European nations meet at the Conference on European Economic Cooperation (CEEC) in Paris.

1949 The Soviets end their blockade of West Berlin.

1950 North Korea invades South Korea; the Korean War begins.

1952 The Marshall Plan is terminated. Aid to Europe is provided through the Mutual Security Program, which includes economic and military support and technical assistance.

1953 George Marshall receives the Nobel Peace Prize for his work in implementing the European Recovery Program (the Marshall Plan).

Glossary

Allies The nations who fought on the same side to defeat Germany during the Second World War were called the Allies; they included France, Great Britain, the USSR, the United States, China, Canada, Australia, and New Zealand.

Axis Germany, Italy, and Japan were three of the most powerful nations fighting the Second World War against the Allies.

balance of power After World War II, the United States and the Soviet Union avoided going to war against each other by maintaining a balance of power in which neither side achieved decisive military superiority.

capitalism An economic and political system in which the central government has only limited control of the nation's trade and industry; in a capitalist system, individuals and businesses are relatively free to make as much profit as they can through their own efforts.

Communism Derived from the writings of German philosopher Karl Marx, Communism is an ideology and an economic and political system that strives to replace a profit-based economy with public or communal ownership, especially of the major means of production and of a country's natural resources, such as forests, waterways, and minerals.

containment The guiding principle of United States foreign policy with respect to the Soviet Union during the years of the Cold War; containment in practice meant impeding Soviet efforts to expand their domain of influence and spread their ideology.

Economic Cooperation Act Signed into law by President Truman on April 3, 1948, this legislation established the European Recovery Program, or the official title of the Marshall Plan.

European Recovery Program Inspired by Secretary of State George Marshall's Harvard commencement address in June 1947, this program, also called the Marshall Program, launched America's comprehensive effort to help Europe recover from the destruction of World War II.

Great Depression Beginning with the stock market crash in 1929 and lasting until the end of the 1930s, the Great Depression was a severe economic decline that drove millions into poverty throughout the world.

infrastructure Physical structures, equipment, and facilities that make it possible for a geographical region (such as a country or state) to function effectively.

Iron Curtain The nonphysical, metaphorical barrier that divided the East and West during the decades of the Cold War.

laisser-faire This French term refers to an economic system in which businesses are free to conduct transactions with minimal government interference or control.

level-of-industry At the conclusion of the Second World War, the Allies imposed a level-of-industry plan on the German economy; the aim of the plan was to keep German industry from exceeding the output of industries in France and other countries that had been at war with Germany.

long telegram Written by the American diplomat George Kennan in 1946 and sent from his office in Moscow to the Department of State, this document presented Kennan's views on the Soviet Union.

Marshall Plan Officially known as the European Recovery Program, the Marshall Plan was a comprehensive aid program aiming to facilitate the integration of European economies while supporting Europe's efforts to recover from the Second World War.

Marxism A political philosophy and ideology that derives from the writings of Karl Marx, a nineteenth century German philosopher and economist who envisioned the defeat of capitalism and the eventual emergence of a classless society.

multilateral Agreements or transactions between three or more parties (individuals, businesses, governments).

plebiscite The direct vote of all electorate members on an important public proposal.

subversive Seeking to disrupt an established system.

Truman Doctrine In his March 1947 speech to Congress, President Truman set forth the principles that would guide United States foreign policy throughout the Cold War, which included supporting any democratic nation at risk of Communist subversion from internal or external threats.

Bibliography

Chomsky, Noam. "Democracy in the Industrial Societies." In *Deterring Democracy*. Cambridge, MA: South End Press, 1991. https://zcomm.org/wp-content/uploads/zbooks/www/chomsky/dd/dd-c11-s02.html.

Hogan, Michael J. *The Marshall Plan: America, Britain, and the Reconstruction of Western Europe, 1947–1952.* New York: Cambridge University Press, 1989.

Lowe, Keith. "Part I: The Legacy of War." In *Savage Continent: Europe in the Aftermath of World War II*, 3-74. New York: St. Martin's Press, 2012.

"The Marshall Plan–'The Europeans did the job themselves.'" Association for Diplomatic Studies and Training. Accessed October 15, 2016. http://adst.org/2015/05/the-marshall-plan-the-europeans-did-the-job-themselves.

McGlinchey, Stephen. "The Marshall Plan, the Truman Doctrine, and the Division of Europe." E-International Relations. October 13, 2009. http://www.e-ir.info/2009/10/13/the-marshall-plan-the-truman-doctrine-and-the-division-of-europe.

Narinsky, Mikhail M., and Scott D. Parrish. "New Evidence on the Soviet Rejection of the Marshall Plan, 1947: Two Reports." Woodrow International Center for Scholars. Accessed October 21, 2016. https://www.wilsoncenter.org/sites/default/files/ACFB73.pdf.

Padoan, Carlo P., and Eliot Sorel, eds. *The Marshall Plan: Lessons Learned for the 21st Century.* Accessed October 4, 2016. http://www.learneurope.eu/files/8113/7509/5720/Plan_Marshall._Lecciones_aprendidas_s_XXI.pdf.

"Quick Study: George Kennan's Cold War Policy of Containment: A Conversation with Kennan's Biographer." *The Economist.* November 28, 2011. http://www.economist.com/blogs/prospero/2011/11/quick-study-george-kennan's-cold-war-policy-containment.

"The Truman Doctrine." Alpha History. Accessed October 15, 2016. http://alphahistory.com/coldwar/truman-doctrine.

"The Truman Doctrine and Marshall Aid." Nationalarchives.gov.uk. Accessed October 5, 2016. http://www.nationalarchives.gov.uk/education/coldwar/G3/cs3.

Zickel, Raymond E., ed. "Soviet Union 1945-1985." In *The Soviet Union: A Country Study.* Washington, DC: Federal Research Division of the Library of Congress, 1989. http://www.shsu.edu/~his_ncp/Soviet2.html.

Further Information

Books

Hogan, Michael J. *The Marshall Plan: America, Britain, and the Reconstruction of Western Europe, 1947–1952*. New York: Cambridge University Press, 1989.

Holm, Michael. *The Marshall Plan: A New Deal for Europe (Critical Moments in American History)*. New York: Routledge, 2016.

Lowe, Keith. *Savage Continent: Europe in the Aftermath of World War II*. New York: St. Martin's Press, 2012.

Mills, Nicolaus. *Winning the Peace: The Marshall Plan and America's Coming of Age as a Superpower.* Hoboken, New Jersey: John Wiley & Sons, Inc., 2008.

Websites

George C. Marshall Foundation

http://marshallfoundation.org/marshall/the-marshall-plan/

This website features a treasure trove of material about George Marshall, including primary sources.

The History Channel

http://www.history.com/topics/world-war-ii/marshall-plan/videos

This website by the History Channel includes videos, speeches, and short biographies of important figures involved in the Marshall Plan.

The Miller Center

http://millercenter.org/president/truman

This site contains information about Truman's presidency and comprehensive articles concerning his foreign and domestic policies.

Videos

The Marshall Plan Speech

https://www.youtube.com/watch?v=dg9_GqXa770

This video from the Marshall Foundation features the voice of George Marshall delivering his June 1947 speech at Harvard University.

The Truman Doctrine

https://www.youtube.com/watch?v=wmQD_W8Pcxg

In this video, viewers can watch President Truman deliver his 1947 speech to Congress and scenes from Greece's civil war that prompted Truman to request an aid package for both Greece and Turkey.

Index

Page numbers in **boldface** are illustrations. Entries in **boldface** are glossary terms.

Allies, 7, 13, 19, 21–22, 42–43, 54, 76, 81
ambassador, 9, 23, 65
Axis, 21, 63

balance of power, 41, 54
Berlin, 16, 19, 21, **26**, 68, 97
"Big Three," 7–8, 20–21, 53

capitalism, 39, 43, 81
Churchill, Winston, 7, 21–22, 28, **30**, 34, 53–54, 56, 63
Communism, 9, 23, 28, 41, 46, 68, 78, 81
Communist, 6, 8, 21–25, 29, 31–34, 41–42, 46, 52, 68, 81, 94–95
Conference on European Economic Cooperation (CEEC), 74, **75**, 76
containment, 23, 25, 66, 69

D-day, **12**, 12–13
Department of State/State Department, 23–24, 43–44, 48–49, 59, 67–68, 90

Eastern Europe, 6, 20–23, 28, 30, 49, 54, 69, 76, 93–95
economic aid, 74, 94–95
Economic Cooperation Act (ECA), 73, 78
European Recovery Program, 36–37, 63, 73, 85
European Union (EU), 81, 90–93, 98

famine, 16, 61, 64
Foreign Assistance Act, 37, 95
foreign policy, 21, 24, 35–36, 51, 53, 94–96
France, 7, 11–13, **12**, 37, 40–43, 49, 52, 60, 63, 81–82, 86, 90

Germany, 7–8, 11–13, 19–21, 24, **26**, 29–30, 40–44, 46, 48–49, 43, 54, 59–60, 63–64, 68, 74, 81, 85–86, 93, 97
Great Britain, 7, 13, 21, 31, 33, 37, 49, 81, 97
Great Depression, **38**, 39, 57, **58**
Greece, 25, 30–31, **32**, 33–35, 41, 52, 88, 90, 94

Hitler, Adolf, 7, 13, 64
Hoover, Herbert, 9, 44, **48**, 57–61, **57**

infrastructure, 39, 46, 51, 80
Iron Curtain, 94

Kennan, George, 9, 23, 25, 45–46, **45**, 48–49, 65–69, **66**, 90, 96
Kremlin, 68, 74

laisser-faire, 39
level-of-industry, 42–44
long telegram, 23, 65, 69

Manhattan Project, 54
Marshall, George, 8–9, 25, 36–37, 41, 45–47, 49, 61–63, **62**, 65, 71–74, 76
Marshall Plan, 8–9, 24, 36–37, 41, 45, **47**, 49, 51, 61, 63, 73–74, 76, 79–83, 85–86, 88–91, 93–94, 96–98
Marxism, 68
Molotov, Vyacheslav, 37, 74–75
multilateral, 40, 90

Normandy, 11–13, **12**
North Atlantic Treaty Organization (NATO), 24

Organization for European Economic Cooperation (OEEC), 76, 89–90

plebiscite, 32
Potsdam Conference, 8, 20–21, 53–54, 56, 65
productivity mission, 82, 89–90

Reagan, Ronald, 23, 66
rebuilding, 9, 20, 22, 33, 39, 40–42, 47, 59, 62, 71, 79, 88, 94
Roosevelt, Franklin D., 7, 21, 28, **30**, 38, 53, 59
Russian Revolution, 9, 31

Stalin, Joseph, 7, 21–22, 28–29, **30**, 33, 53–54, 56, 68–69
subversive, 9

Treaty of Rome, **92**, 93
Truman, Harry S., 7–9, 21–22, 24–25, 33, 35–37, **35**, 40, 42, 44, 48, **50**, 51–56, 59, 65, 69, 73, 94–96
Truman Doctrine, 9, 24, 33, 36, 51, 94, 96–97
Turkey, 33, 35, 52, 94

Union of Soviet Socialist Republics (USSR), 5–6, 27, 41

V-J Day, 17, **18**

War Department, 43–44, 48, 59, 65
Western Europe, 8, 22–23, 40, 49, 72, 78, 80, 86, 90, 92, 96
Wilson, Woodrow, 60–61
World War I/First World War, 38–39, 52, 63, 81
World War II/Second World War, 7, **12**, **14**, 16, 24, 28, 36,44, 51, 59, 61, 69, 71, 85–86, 97

Yalta Conference, 7, 21, 28, 65

About the Author

George Capaccio is the author of several books of historical nonfiction for students. George has also researched and written about topics in science and health. His publishing credits in these fields feature books about ADHD, cancer treatments, the digestive and nervous systems, and books about Mars, Jupiter, and the Sun. George is also a poet and professional storyteller. After researching the life and work of Albert Einstein, he created an original monologue, which he performs in the person of Einstein for schools, libraries, senior living communities, and other venues. George and his wife Nancy live in Arlington, Massachusetts with their golden retriever, Sasha.